# SPOIL THE CHILD, DESTROY THE NATION

A Collection Of Sixteen Nigerian Plays That Depict The National And Family Values

'Dipo Toby Alakija

© **Copyright 2018 by Dipo Toby Alakija.**

All rights reserved by Calvary Rock Publishing And Christian Education And Ministration Services (CEMS) in Nigeria. No part of this book may be reproduced or transmitted in any form or by any means without written permission of the publisher through any of the addresses below, apart from the use of short quotations or occasional page copying for personal or group study.

ISBN: 978-9783571464
ISBN: 978357146X


**Printed in United States**
Published by the publishing house of

## CALVARY ROCK PUBLISHING
19, Ajina Street, Ikenne Remo,
Ogun State,
Nigeria.

36, Thomson road
Gorton
Manchester
M18 7QQ
United Kingdom

www.calvaryrock.org

# SPOIL THE CHILD, SPOIL THE NATION

A Collection Of Sixteen Nigerian Plays That Depict The National And Family Values

| Play Title | Page |
|---|---|
| Spoil The Child, Spoil The Nation | 1 |
| Spoil The Child, Destroy His Life | 11 |
| Aggression From Home To school | 21 |
| Vices Begin At Home | 28 |
| The Beast In The Child | 43 |
| The Abuse Of Young Generation | 55 |
| "I Pledge To Nigeria; My Country" | 65 |
| Abused Mother Abuses Her Child | 73 |
| Enticement Into Sex Slavery | 82 |
| Three Deadly Things About Life | 95 |
| Agents Of Corruption | 101 |
| Life Of Darkness On Campus | 112 |
| Harvest Of Bad Seed | 132 |
| The Walking Dead | 141 |
| The Father Of The Beast | 149 |
| The Melodiously Bad Influence | 157 |

Written By
**DIPO TOBY ALAKIJA**

# SPOIL THE CHILD, SPOIL THE NATION

## SCENE ONE A

*(Dr katty walks to the podium in the hall as the melody of "It Doesn't Matter" begins.)*

**MELODY:** *It doesn't matter who owns the idea as long as it is good*
*It doesn't matter if it is not popular as long as it makes sense*
*It doesn't matter if it is unpleasant as long as it is right*
*It doesn't matter if it is bitter As long as it is the truth....*

**DR KATHY:** *(speaks, using the microphone.)* First of all, I will like to give God all the glory for bringing us together to talk about the National Values. This paper is not academic but an educative and informative presentation that is aimed at unveiling the truth about the state of our nation and possibly to make all adults understand the fact that some parents contribute to the problems of this country through the way they raise their children. For this reason I would be using few cases to establish the truth. *(She pauses briefly, moving closer to the people in the hall. She stands in their midst, looking round and smiling at them.)* The adage which says that "charity begins at home" establishes the fact that whatever is going on in the society begins at individual homes ... I remember when I was a Counsellor in a Secondary School some years ago, there was a boy who was spoilt by his parents because he was their only child. He was so pampered that he has his own driver who would take him to school since the time he began his education up to the time he was admitted into the Secondary School where I was the Counsellor then. When I observed the trend of his life through his conduct and activities in the school, I called him into my office to advise him about his life...

## SCENE TWO

*(Dr Kathy sits in the office, jotting some things on the paper as the melody continues.)*

**MELODY:** *It doesn't matter if it is ugly*
*as long as it is pure*
*It doesn't matter if it is unbelievable*
*As long as it is a fact....*

**DR KATHY:** *(There is a knock on the door.)* You can come in, Omo Nla....

**OMO NLA:** *(opens the door with two other boys, standing with him.)* Good day Counsellor! *(He looks cheerfully round the office, waving at the place.)* This is not a bad office at all but I can tell my dad to help you give it a face lift.

**DR KATHY:** That wont be necessary, Omo Nla. *(She looks at the other two boys who greet her by bowing a little.)* What are you boys doing here?

**OMO NLA:** I told them to follow me down here.

**DR. KATHY:** *(waves at the door.)* Get out of here, boys! *(The two boys leave the office immediately. She looks at Omo Nla.)* I told only you to see me. Why coming here with those boys? Are they your body guards or something?

**OMO NLA:** Take it easy, Mama me. They are my friends.

**DR. KATHY:** *(looks annoyed as she silently gestures him to sit on the chair in front of her. Omo Nla looks reluctant. She shouts at him.)* Sit down, young man! *(He sits down on the chair slowly. She stands up and begin to pace round in front of him at the back of her seat.)* There was a song my teacher taught us in class when I was your age. The teacher composed it....

**OMO NLA:** *(chuckles.)* It must be an old school stuff, isn't it?

**DR KATHY:** Keep quiet! *(She moves closer and glares at him.)* Who do you imagine yourself to be - the son of the world President who can do anything he likes and go away with it? Think of what you are doing to yourself for a second!

**OMO NLA:** I thought you want to sing an old song to me - ma…

**DR KATHY:** *(sighs.)* Okay, let me recite the lyrics to you before I tell you the mess you are making out of your life.

**OMO NLA:** *(frowns.)* Mess? What do you mean by that?

**DR. KATHY:** You keep your big mouth shut and let me do the talking, okay? ***(He shrugs indifferently.)*** That's better. ***(She begins to recite the lyrics.)*** Life is a very serious game. Don't play it with levity. Even though life is a challenge, it can make you a real champion. At times life can be so bitter even though it can be made sweet.... ***(She pauses, looking at him.)*** Do you find any sense in the lyrics?

**OMO NLA:** *(shrugs.)* No, ma. I don't.

**DR. KATHY:** *(frowns at him.)* You mean you don't get the message in the song? ***(He looks indifferently, shaking his head silently. She goes back to her seat and stares at him.)*** I know you're not retarded. So I expect you to get the message... In any case, I'll explain it to you if you don't understand it.

**OMO NLA:** *(looks a little impatient.)* Can I come again some other time? I've got some things to do.

**DR. KATHY:** *(in a harsh tone.)* No! What I'm about to tell you is much more important than whatever you want to do. It is important to you, your parents and the society. So you better listen to me!

**OMO NLA:** Okay. I'm all ears...

**DR. KATHY:** Life is a very serious game means that life is full of games, some of which are so serious and dangerous that they can claim your life if you don't play the game well enough by doing the right thing every time. Because of this you can not afford to play the games of life carelessly. ***(She stares hard at his indifferent expression before she continues.)*** With the way you are playing the games of life in the school, throwing money around; going to parties, messing

around with girls and - all kinds of life....
**OMO NLA:** *(looks puzzled.)* Who told you all that?
**DR. KATHY:** That shouldn't be the question. The real question is: is it true or not?
**OMO NLA:** I know who told you all that.
**DR KATHY:** You don't need to suspect anyone. I know how to get my facts about everyone in the school. What I just want to tell you is this: with the way you're living, you made wind up getting involved with crime which can inevitably claim your life....

## SCENE ONE B

**DR KATHY:** ...The boy went home to say all sorts of bad things about me to his parents, telling them what I didn't say....

## SCENE THREE

*(Omo Nla is with Atiba and Mamadi in the well furnished sitting room as the melody continues.)*
**MELODY:** *It doesn't matter how much the sacrifice*
*as long as it is for the benefit of all*
*It doesn't matter how people react to it*
*as long as it is the truth....*
**OMO NLA:** ... Dad, mum, if you hear what the School Counsellor told me today, you would have her fired.
**ATIBA:** *(looks interested.)* What did she say to you?
**OMO NLA:** She said I'm growing into criminal.... I'm spoilt from home... and I may die a criminal....
**MAMADI:** *(looks puzzled.)* What? **(She looks at Atiba who looks angry.)**
**ATIBA:** Are you sure of this?
**OMO NLA:** Yes, dad. Why should I lie about it? I knew she was going to deny this if you ask her. That's the reason she told my friends who went with me to leave her office. She called them my body guards....

## SCENE ONE C

**DR KATHY:** ... The parents went to report me to the principal the following day. I was invited to meet them at the Principal's office....

## SCENE FOUR

*(Principal, Dr Kathy, Atiba and Mamadi are in the office.)*

**PRINCIPAL:** .... The boy said you called him a criminal who would soon die...

**DR KATHY:** That's not what I said ...all he told you are all lies.

**ATIBA:** Why did you drive away his friends who could serve as witnesses?

**DR KATHY:** Mr Atiba...

**ATIBA:** *(looks offended.)* I am Chief Atiba,

**DR KATHY:** I'm sorry. I didn't know you're a Chief. Anyway, I don't really expect you to come here and accuse me of calling your son names. Even if I did, what I expect from you is to ask me why I have to talk to your son. If you ask me that, I would say your son is growing out of hand. With the way he was brought up, he feels he can do whatever he wants and get anything he wants... I meant to tell him that life is not designed that way. I wanted to teach him the way he should live his life.

**MAMADI:** Perhaps you should teach us the way he should live his life since you're the only one who knows.

**ATIBA:** Oh, yes! We are in the classroom now. You can deliver your lecture.

**PRINCIPAL:** Chief Atiba, please, I'm sorry for all these....

**DR. KATHY:** *(looks offended.)* You are sorry for what? They should be apologizing to me! It was the boy who insulted me for trying to do my job.

**PRINCIPAL:** Miss Kathy, take it easy.

**DR. KATHY:** Sir, I'm trying to do my job here. Instead of them to support me, they are here to insult me as well. *(She looks at Atiba and Mamadi.)* If you must know, I represent the interest of other parents and the nation at large. *(She stares hard at them.)* Going by my training before I was attached to this School as a Counselor, I see the sighs of potentials of a cult guy in your son if at all he is not yet one. With what I see in him, if he gets to tertiary institutions, cultist will compete with one another to get him initiated as one of their members. *(She smiles at them when they frown.)* You want me to deliver the lecture now? I will be obliged to do that. Going by the research of the character building organization I work for, all secret cults on campuses in Nigeria are always on the look out for people who will fund their vice rings. With the way your son is throwing money around, he would be one of their targets. Secondly, you didn't teach your son the legitimate way of making money. Instead, you are teaching him how to waste money. As a good businessman, I don't need to tell you that if your son keep wasting money like, you make him a liability instead of an asset in your business. Apart from that, if there is no money to throw around again, he would begin to look for any means to make money, including going diabolical. This is how vices begin at home. I'm trying to prevent this and you are here to tell annoying things. *(She stands up, looking at Principal.)* I need to see a change in the boy's attitude otherwise I would be forced to report this case to the Commissioner For Education. *(She leaves the office.)*

## SCENE ONE D

**DR KATHY:** ... I did not know the boy already has a gang and I don't know what the Principal told the parents but my guess is that he made all my points clearer to them. Whatever could have happened, the parents must have tried to call the boy to order but it was too late. Before I tell you what happened next, I have point out a few things to parents and teachers. Four things primarily constitute the Nigerian National Value System. One of them is the Family Values. This is a set of belief within the nuclear or extended family. It provides the training ground for children to become responsible or irresponsible. For this reason, the adage says that charity begins at home.

The second thing that constitutes the National Value System is the Traditional Values, which is the set of beliefs, norms and cultures that are peculiar to a particular community or ethnic group of people.

The third is the Moral or Religious Values. The use of the two words are deliberate to connote that Religion without morals can become so barbaric to the point of killing fellow human beings. Thus for any religion to serve the purpose of National Values, there must be some morals embedded in it.

The fourth one is the main framework of the National Value System that is embedded in The National Anthem and The Pledge To Nigeria. The two recognize the fact that there must be some beliefs in the God of creation, which will make the people God-fearing before the people can be morally sound.

All these four things must be in harmony before the Value System can work effectively even at the local level. If any one of them fails to work - say like the case we are treating now, there would be problem that may affect the entire society. *(She pauses briefly before she smiles.)* Let me now continue or round up the story of Omo Nla... As I said, it was too late for his parents to curb his excesses. The next thing he did to me for attempting to correct him was to send his gang attack me.... *(Many of the people look puzzled.)*

## SCENE FIVE

*(The melody continues as Dr Kathy drives along the road.)*

**MELODY:** *It does not matter what anyone may say*
*as long as it is what God says*
*It does not matter how you voice it as long*
*as you express what is right....*

*(Some youths block her way and command her to park the car. Then they order her to get down.)*

**1st YOUTH:** We've not come to kill you but to teach you the lesson you will not forget in your life.

**DR KATHY:** ... W-w-w- what did I do?
**2nd YOUTH:** You are poking your pussy cat nose into the matter that does not concern you!
**3rd YOUTH:** If not that you're too old for us, we would have dragged you somewhere and rape you.
**DR KATHY:** Please, don't hurt me... I was only trying to help you, guys....
**1st YOUTH:** Why wasting time talking with this old pussy cat? Let's deal with her. ***(They begin to beat until she faints. The youths then run away.)***

## SCENE ONE E

**DR KATHY:** ... That day was one of the worst days of my life. I woke up in the hospital the following day. Since then I was not bold enough to help the youths in the school until the organization replaced me with someone else. More often than not, most parents are parts of those what make our jobs as School Counsellors difficult. If things parents teach their children are different from what we teach them, they make the job impossible. If they also neglect their responsibilities to their children, they simply make their homes training ground where criminals are bred. If children are spoilt, the nation would be at risk of vices and crimes in future. Let us view it this way: rich parents mandate drivers take their children to schools and bring them back home and provide everything the children request for, ranging from choice food, choice toys and cable t.v programmes. The children are exposed to only luxuries of life. They are not exposed to anything rigorous. They have no rules to follow, no pains to feel, no challenges to face. He goes to tertiary institution and continues to live like that. When they graduate, what kind of work do we expect them to do? They will find it hard to be productive because they are not trained to be productive. It may get to a point of planning the deaths of their parents so that they can inherit their properties. It is then that parents will realize that they were breeding wild lions, thinking they are caring for them. Bible says in Proverb 22:6 says that we should train a child in the way he should go. When he is old, he will not depart from it. Proverb 23:6 also says that we should not withhold correction from children. If we beat them with canes, they will not die. The two wise sayings make us to know that we have to tutor and culture the young ones if we really love them. By teaching them right ways of life, we are actually helping them and the nation at large....

# SPOIL THE CHILD, DESTROY HIS LIFE

## SCENE ONE

*(The melody begins as Lawyer drives into Atiba's compound.)*

**MELODY:** *Life is a very serious game*
*Don't play it with levity*
*Even though life is a challenge, it*
*can make you a champion...*

*(He parks in front of the house. He gets out and walks briskly towards the house.)*

*At times life can be so bitter*
*Even though it can be made sweet*
*Life can be so hard on anyone that*
*Only few can break through*
*Life can be so frustrating*
*that it can lead to insanity....*

*(The house keeper opens the door and waits for him to move closer to her.)*

**HOUSE KEEPER:** You're welcome, sir.

**LAWYER:** Thank you very much... Chief Atiba must have been waiting for me.

**HOUSE KEEPER:** That's true, sir, but he understands you are always so busy... Please, come inside... *(She steps aside for him to enter the sitting room.)* This way, please...

**LAWYER:** Thank you… *(The melody continues.)*

**MELODY:** *Life can be wonderful only if it*
*is filled with Spirit of God*
*Life can be nothing to some because it*
*is full of sorrow*
*Life can be filled with peace and joy*
*only when God is in control*
*Life can be reaction of whatever you*
*put inside....*

## SCENE TWO A

*(Atiba and Lawyer are in the sitting room, talking.)*

**LAWYER:** ... But Chief I don't understand the reason you

want to will all your properties to the character building organization when you have a son. It sounds weird to me...

**ATIBA:** *(looks a little depressed.)* I don't have a son.

**LAWYER:** *(frowns.)* How about Omo Nla?

**ATIBA:** *(sighs deeply, looking very thoughtful for a long time before he whispers.)* Omo Nla died a long time ago.

**LAWYER:** *(looks puzzled the more.)* What does that mean if I may ask, sir?

**ATIBA:** *(sighs again.)* Physically he may be alive but deep inside me he is dead. My wife and I killed him when he was a child.

**LAWYER:** You're speaking in riddles. Can you please explain everything to me, sir?

**ATIBA:** I will if you have the time.

**LAWYER:** I'm giving you the rest of the day. Once I leave this place, I'm going straight home unless you give me reasons I have to go back to the office.

**ATIBA:** *(hesitates for a while.)* Yeah, you will have to go back to your chamber and prepare the papers to sign. ***(He takes a piece of paper on the table and hands it to him.)*** You will need to insert the name of this organization in all the papers. The organization is the one that tried to reform Omo Nla when he was in Secondary School.

**LAWYER:** *(looks at the paper with puzzled expressions. He looks at him again after a while.)* This must be a serious and urgent matter.

**ATIBA:** Yes, it is. I have to act now because I may depart from this world any time. I don't want the evil I have created to continue after I'm dead.

**LAWYER:** You really have to tell me what is happening, sir. If you tell me I may be able advise you or I may be in a better position to understand what you are trying to do.

**ATIBA:** *(nods silently and sighs.)* Okay I'll tell you. I'll make the long story as brief as possible. ***(He stands up slowly and begins to pace up and down in front of***

*him.)* When I got married, my wife could not get pregnant. It took us almost eight years before we could have one. So we technically turned the child into an idol - I mean - object of worship. He was spoilt rotten. We didn't know we were destroying his life while thinking we were caring for him until it was too late. His school Counsellor invited him to her office and counselled him but he came home that day to tell us different thing...

## SCENE THREE
### (Flashback)

**OMO NLA:** ... Dad, mum, if you hear what the School Counsellor told me today, you would have her fired.

**ATIBA:** *(looks interested.)* What did she say to you?

**OMO NLA:** She said I'm growing into criminal.... I'm spoilt from home... and I may die a criminal....

**MAMADI:** *(looks puzzled.)* What? *(She looks at Atiba who looks angry.)*

**ATIBA:** Are you sure of this?

**OMO NLA:** Yes, dad. Why should I lie about this? I knew she was going to deny this if you ask her. That's the reason she told my friends to leave her office. She called them my body guards…

## SCENE TWO B

**ATIBA:** ...Instead of me and my wife to find out what exactly the Councellor observed before she decided to talk to Omo Nla and call him to order, we reported her to the Principal who was always on our side even if we do anything wrong. He was always on our side because he thought we're generous people who donate a lot into the school projects. We had the mind to use our influence get the Counsellor dismissed as Omo Nla desired. We could not do that, not because she was not a Government officer but because she told us some truths...

## SCENE FOUR
### (Flashback)
*(Principal, Dr Kathy, Atiba and Mamadi are in the office.)*
**PRINCIPAL:** Chief Atiba, please, I'm sorry for all these….
**DR. KATHY:** *(looks offended.)* You are sorry for what? They should be apologizing to me! It was the boy who insulted me for trying to do my job.
**PRINCIPAL:** Miss Kathy, take it easy.
**DR. KATHY:** Sir, I'm trying to do my job here. Instead of them to support me, they are here to insult me as well. *(She looks at Atiba and Mamadi.)* If you must know, I represent the interest of other parents and the nation at large. *(She stares hard at them.)* Going by my training before I was attached to this School as a Counsellor, I see the sighs of potentials of a cult guy in your son if at all he is not yet one. With what I see in him, if he gets to tertiary institutions, cultist will compete with one another to get him initiated as one of their members….

## SCENE TWO C
**ATIBA:** As at that time, it was getting too late, if not too late to control Omo Nla. He went as far as arranging boys to beat up the poor Counsellor up to the point of landing in the hospital on admission. *(Lawyer looks puzzled.)* We did not know this until the Counsellor was replaced with another one who ensured that Omola Nla was expelled from school. One the reasons I want to will all my properties to the organization is the boldness of its officials and the risks they always take to reform children were deformed at homes. It was the case of my son that makes me realize how risky it is to reform people whose characters were deformed by parents like me and my wife. *(He pauses again, looking thoughtful.)* … The truths which the former Counsellor told us back then turned out to be

prophesies of what we were yet to experience. We did not know how much havoc we have wrecked on the boy's life until he got to the University. If again, we have followed the truths we were told, we were not supposed to let him get close to the entrance of the University. As the Counsellor tried to point to us, the pressure or influence of different characters on campus is not something Omola Nla could possibly resist, aside from the fact we didn't lay a good foundation for him. He became member of secret cults on campus. He was always asking large sum of money from me. We didn't know he was using it to fund the secret cult until he was arrested with some other students who were involved in cult conflicts. Still hoping to rehabilitate him, we managed to get him out and brought him home....

## SCENE FIVE

*(Omo Nla, dressed all in black with the image of a skull and crossed bones stands in front of Abita and Mamadi who both sit on the couch.)*

**ATIBA:** ... You expect us to believe you were coerced to become a member of a secret cult?

**OMO NLA:** *(looks innocent.)* Yes, dad!

**MAMADI:** Tell us how you were coerced.

**OMO NLA:** It was one of my course mate who invited me to a meeting of a group in the night... I didn't know it is a secret cult.

**ATIBA:** *(springs up suddenly.)* Did you hear yourself? You were invited to a meeting at night. This only establish the fact that he who is taught evil and follows it has some elements of evil inside of him.

**MAMADI:** *(stands up and moves close to Atiba.)* You know most of the Nigerian Universities are full of secret cults. It's the Government's responsibility to ensure that the places of learning are conducive for students... Let's take him to another University since he has leant his lesson in the hands of the police....

## SCENE TWO D

**ATIBA:**.... We changed the school as my wife said but instead of the situation to improve, he grew worse. He not only get involved in secret cult, he also takes hard drugs. It was when we discovered this that we realized that we're responsible for the kind of life he has chosen. We have laid a terribly bad foundation for him....

## SCENE SIX

*(Melody continues as Omo Nla takes hard drug in the room.)*

**MELODY:** *Life is so important to everyone*
*that it determines eternity*
*Life may take some years to end*
*yet it can end at any time....*

*(Mamadi opens the door without knocking and enters the room. She looks shocked when she sees Omo Nla taking hard drugs.)*

**MAMADI:** *(waves at the drugs on the table.)* Oh, my God! What's this?

**OMO NLA:** *(looks startled to see her.)* It's ... some... em... pain killers, mum.

**MAMADI:** *(moves closer to examine the contents, looking frantic.)* Pain killer? *(She takes some of white substance and puts it on her left palm.)* I'll find out before I believe you.

**OMO NLA:** *(looks offended.)* Where are you taking it to?

**MAMADI:** I'm going to find out if this thing is pain killer or something else.

**OMO NLA:** How are you going to do that?

**MAMADI:** You don't have to worry about that.

## SCENE TWO E

**ATIBA:** ... His mother was the one who discovered that he is a drug addict. When I challenged him, his reaction proved it to us that we've been raising a wild animal who is a threat in the house.

## SCENE SEVEN

*(Atiba and Omo Nla stand in the sitting room, facing each other as they argue while Mamadi looks at them with depression.)*

**ATIBA:** This explains reasons you always misbehave. You are a drug addict.

**OMO NLA:** Who told you I'm a drug addict? *(He looks at Mamadi.)* I told you the drug is pain killer....

**MAMADI:** The drug is confirmed cocaine! So give us another story!

**OMO NLA:** You're being unreasonable!

**ATIBA:** *(looks puzzled.)* What? How dare you say that to your mother!

**OMO NLA:** *(glares at him.)* What have I said, old man? *(His parents look at him with disbelief.)* You guys better get ready to die because I'm ready to take over your properties. After all, you have no one who can inherit your properties except me.

**ATIBA:** *(exchanges glances with Mamadi.)* Y-you're telling us to die!

**OMO NLA:** Yeah, old man. If you don't die easy way, you'll die hard way! *(**He leaves the sitting room immediately. Mamadi burst into hysterical sobs.**)*

## SCENE TWO F

**ATIBA:** ... Since that day my wife started dying slowly. But she took refuge in studying the Bible, using it to comfort herself ....

## SCENE EIGHT

*(Mamadi reads the Bible in the sitting room as the melody continues.)*

**MELODY:** *Life has nothing much to offer unless it is given up to Christ....*

*(Atiba enters the sitting room and goes to sit beside her on the couch, putting his arm round her shoulder.*

*She attempts to smile at him. She bursts into sobs.)*

**ATIBA:** …. It's okay honey, I don't expect you to feel this way since you've given your life to Christ. *(He withdraws his hand and looks at her with smiles.)*

**MAMADI:** It's true that if we don't train a child, we give room for his destruction... I can't stop feeling so guilty that I'm responsible for the perverted ways of life of our son...

**ATIBA:** It's a mistake we've made. Only God can put his life back to normal… We didn't give him the training he can fall back on when he missed the right way. That is the reason he moves from one error right into another, one wrong step into another one, which is leading him to destruction.

**MAMADI:** Yes. *(There is silence.)* One of my concerns are the victims of his atrocities. We know few of his victims like the School Counsellor. There must be many others who are hurt or killed.

**ATIBA:** *(looks thoughtful.)* You're right... *(He sighs.)* I guess there is nothing we can do about it now.

**MAMADI:** There is always something we can do. If Omo Nla can hurt his Counsellor who was trying to help him at the time he was in Secondary School, we can as well imagine what he would have done to anyone who steps on his toes. *(He nods thoughtfully.)* Besides that, imagine him telling us to die so that he can inherit our properties... That's a proof that if he inherits the properties, he will cause more harms... *(She looks thoughtful.)* I think we have to let him know that there is something else we can do with the properties... Let us will the properties to the character building organization that tried to reform him when he was in Secondary School...

**ATIBA:** *(nods thoughtfully.)* That's makes sense...

## SCENE TWO G

**ATIBA:** …. My wife traced the organization before she

died.... *(Lawyer looks a little depressed.)* You can now see the basis of willing the properties to the organization. *(He goes to sit down again.)*
**LAWYER:** I can see your reason now....

## SCENE NINE

*(About two years later, Omo Nla is with Lawyer in the office, looking furious.)*

**OMO NLA:** You mean my late father willed all the properties to a charity organization?

**LAWYER:** Yes, I'm sorry. If you have problem with that, you can go to court.

**OMO NLA:** *(grins with anger.)* Do you realize somebody is going to pay heavily for this?

**LAWYER:** I wonder who is going to pay.

**OMO NLA:** *(looks furious.)* You, moron! Unless you do something about getting my properties back, you'll be dead!

**LAWYER:** Even if you kill me, it can never change a thing because your father have already given the properties to the organization before he died. He only told me to do the legal paper works, which I have done. It's the organization and the court you're to deal with if you have any issue, not me...

**OMO NLA:** *(screams.)* Oh shit!

## SCENE TEN

*(Omo Nla walks dejectedly towards a tree in Atiba's compound, holding a rope in his hand as the melody continues.)*

**MELODY:** *Life is a serious game*
*Don't play it with levity....*

*(He climbs the tree slowly and then ties the rope round one of the branches. He ties a knot round his neck with the rope and hangs himself.)*

# TRANSFER OF AGGRESSION FROM HOME TO SCHOOL

## SCENE ONE

*(Fiyani walks towards the office of the Secondary School Counsellor, holding his bag as the melody of "I did not know" begins.)*

**MELODY:** *I did not know the world is a battlefield*
*until I see bloodshed all around me*
*I did not know I was surrounded with enemies*
*until I was struck at the back by a friend ...*

*(He pauses at the entrance of the office and knocks.)*

## SCENE TWO

*(Counsellor stands by the bookshelf in her office, looking through the pages of the book she is holding when there is a knock. She glances at the door before going to take her seat behind her desk.)*

**COUNSELCOR:** Who is it?

**FIYANI:** It's Fiyani Agbemi, ma.

**COUNSELLOR:** You can come inside. *(Fiyani opens the door, murmurs a greeting and bows.)* What takes you so long?

**FIYANI:** I'm sorry, ma. I... em... I was taking some meal...

**COUNSELLOR:** I know you don't want to meet me again.

**FIYANI:** That's not true, ma...

**COUNSELLOR:** *(snaps.)* Sit down. *(He sits down slowly.)* Whatever I do or say to you is for your own good. *(She brings out a file and opens it.)* From the information I get from you and the school, you're from a Christian background. Am I right? *(He nods silently.)* You don't particularly appreciate your father.

**FIYANI:** I said I don't like him.

**COUNSELLOR:** I told you never to say that. *(There is silence.)* You're going to become a father too, you remember that. You have to be careful with what you say about your father. Besides that the Bible said that you should honour your parents so that you can live long. What makes you feel like that about your father doesn't justify you breaking the law of God. Do you understand? *(He nods slowly.)* Good. Going by complaints about your family, the only way you can help them is to pray for them and focus on your studies. Your parents are living their own lives and you've got your own life to live as well.*(She looks at the file again.)* I have it here that you were once an easy going person until you got to Senior Secondary School. Can you explain the reason for this change?

**FINANI:** I told you, it's my father. He keeps beating my mother for no reason.

**COUNSELLOR:** *(sighs.)* I would like to see your parents.

**FIYANI:** No, ma, please.

**COUNCELOR:** *(frowns at him.)* Why?

**FIYANI:** My father will know I report him to the school.

**COUNSELLOR:** You didn't report him to the school. The violence in your home is extending to the school. *(She sighs again.)* Fiyani, it's my job as the School Counsellor to help you succeed in life. You either allow me to see your parent or I will recommend you to be expelled if you're involved in any violence in school.

**FIYANI:** I promise you I'll not be involved in any violence in the school again.

**COUNSELLOR:** Okay, then. You can go. *(Fiyani leaves the office.)*

## SCENE THREE

*(A few weeks later, Mike and Kemi, Fiyani's parents argue in the sitting room as Fiyani and his sisters prepare to go to school. The melody continues.)*

**MELODY:** *I did not know how I got into trouble*
*until I found myself begging for help*
*I did not know how much I need the Lord*
*until I was getting close to my grave.*

**KEMI:** You're such an irresponsible husband and father!

**MIKE:** God damn your parents for saying that to me!

**KEMI:** God damn your entire family! *(Mike looks furious. He slaps her across the face and bounce on her, beating her. Fiyani looks angry while his sisters* *burst into cries. The melody continues as Fiyani takes them out of the house. Mike punches kemi on the face. She falls on her back, sitting up quickly to protect her face as he continues to punch her. Fiyani later comes to join them again and finds kemi, pleading; sobbing and bleeding.)*

**MIKE**: *(growls at her.)* That'll teach you never to look into my face when I'm talking, let alone provoking me!

**FIYANI**: *(in a tough voice.)* Why do you want to kill my mother?

**MIKE**: *(looks surprised.)* What did you say?

**FIYANI**: I say why do you want to kill my mother?

**MIKE**: You had the guts to repeat that. *(He chases Fiyani who quickly runs away from him.)*

**KEMI**: You leave the boy out of this, please...!

**MIKE**: *(continues to run after him in the sitting room until he catches him.)* I'll kill you today! *(He begins to beat him.)*

**KEMI**: Please, don't hurt the boy. I'm begging you in the name of the Lord. *(Fiyani gets the chance to move close to the door. He opens it and looks at Mike with fury.)*

**FIYANI**: I'll go and join the secret cult. I'll mobilize them to come after your life - you murderer! *(He runs out of the house, making his parents look horrified.)*

## SCENE FOUR

*(Fiyani sits in front of the school Counsellor, crying.)*

**FIYANI**: I... I don't want to be a bad boy but my father is making me... I'm sorry I broke the promise I made to you.

**COUNSELLOR**: Do you actually plan to join the secret cult? *(He nods silently.)* Why?

**FIYANI**: *(looks a little surprised at the question.)* I want to use the cult to punish my father for what he did to my mother. I don't really care what did to me. It's painful to see my mother to be punched like that. She was covered with b-blood... She even tried to save me

from him... *(He starts sobbing again.)*
COUNSELLOR: *(stands up to go and part him on the shoulder.)* It's okay, Fiyani. *(She goes to sit down again.)* The implication of going to join any bad gang goes beyond taking revenge against your father. *(He looks puzzled.)* Yes, it's much more than what you think. In fact, the side effect is so deadly that it can cost you your life and lives of many others.
FIYANI: How else can I stop my father from maltreating my mother? I fear I'll kill him one day if he doesn't stop treating her like that.
COUNSELLOR: Fiyani, you must understand that whatever you do to any of your parents is what your children will do to you. I thought you said you are a Christian. You must have read that in your Bible. *(There is silence.)* At this stage of the problem, I'll have to talk to your parents. Is that okay? *(He nods.)* When can I find your father at home?
FIYANI: He comes home after office hours to take his food before he goes out again.

## SCENE FIVE

*(The melody continues while Counsellor and kemi are in the sitting room, talking. Counsellor occasionally takes the fruit drinks in front of her. Mike comes out of the room to join the women.)*
MIKE: *(sits opposite the women who sit together on the couch. He looks at Counsellor.)* Sorry for keeping you waiting.
COUNSELLOR: Oh, there is no need for that, sir. As a matter of fact, I am supposed to thank you for granting me your audience.
MIKE: That's all right. You have all my attention now.
COUNSELLOR: *(bows slightly.)* Thank you, sir. *(She sighs.)* As I told you, I came in respect of the case of your son, Fiyani. You can say I'm representing the interest of the school, your interest and the interest of other parents. *(She pauses for a while.)* When Fiyani

was in Junior Secondary School, he was a cool headed boy. When he gets to Senior Secondary School, however, he began to exhibit some violent traits by picking quarrels over minor things. His case was transferred to the School Counselling Section which is my area. My investigation reveals that he has built up an aggression in the home which is transferred to other students in the school. I tried to see you before now but he declined and promised to change. He came to me yesterday and told me what happened. What made me come to see you so soon was his idea of joining the secret cult.

**MIKE:** *(grins.)* I suppose you need my permission to hand him over to the Police or social welfare.

**COUNSELLOR:** No, sir. That's not what I come for. The fact is: if the boy is reported, you'll be implicated because you caused him to behave like that?

**MIKE:** *(frowns.)* How do you mean?

**COUNSELLOR:** If you were to be in US or UK, with what has happened yesterday, you'll be in jail for criminal assault and child abuse.

**MIKE:** Well, we are not in UK or US. We are in Nigeria where no one tells you how to run your home.

**COUNSELLOR:** *(interrupts.)* With due respect, sir, if I report you to the Police even here in Nigeria, you'll be arrested for the same offences. But I don't believe that's the solution. The solution is that you'll need to change your attitude and care for your family. Failure to do that may cause your own son to arrange youths to waste your life. If that's what you want, you can shun my advice then. With my experiences on issues like this, you can never tell how the conflict is going to end. I have witnessed a situation where a son poured acid on his father's face. *(Mike and Kemi look a little puzzled.)* Yes, sir. That's what I'm trying to point out. You see, sir, family life is not about one person. It's about God at the centre of everything you do. Your wife and your children are the second and third in your list of priorities. Your interest comes last. If your family life is not arranged in that order of priorities, you'll see that you'll build a world round yourself alone. When it falls, it falls only on you. *(She pauses to study his face as he looks thoughtful.)* That's all I can say to you for now. *(She looks at kemi.)* As for you, madam, you have enormous responsibility. You need to see your husband more as your father than your son. Your family life must be in the same order of priority. God first, your husband and children come second and third while your interest comes last. When you start thinking only of yourself by saying "my feelings"; "my children"; "my money", you'll become selfish. Selflessness is the worst part of human character. It makes us lack considerations for others. So whatever goes on in the home whether good or bad is attributed to you - the wife and mother…

## SCENE SIX

*(Mike, Kemi, Fiyani and his sisters are by the dining table. All except Mike who looks thoughtful are taking their meals.)*

**KEMI:** *(looks at Mike.)* Honey, you're not eating your food.

**MIKE:** *(glances at her and sighs.)* I… em… *(He shakes his head.)*

**FIYANI:** *(goes to kneel beside Mike.)* I'm sorry, dad…

**MIKE:** *(lays his hand on his shoulder.)* I'm supposed to say I'm sorry to you. *(He looks round at the rest who stare at them.)* I am sorry for what I have done to all of you in this house. Please, find it in your hearts to forgive me. *(Kemi and the rest move to his side, trying to hug him.)*

**KEMI:** Let's have a good time with the meal… *(She looks at Mike.)* Shall we, honey? We'll talk about this later.

**MIKE:** *(smiles.)* Oh, sure, Mum… *(The rest laugh as they take their meal.)*

# VICES BEGIN AT HOME

## SCENE ONE

*(Pastor drives into the school premises as melody of "Give Me The Grace" begins.)*

**MELODY:** *Give me the grace to stand*
*When others are falling, oh Lord*
*Give me the strength to sail the ocean*
*When others are getting drown….*

*(Miss Benson who waits by the entrance of the hall hurries to meet Pastor.)*

**MISS BENSON:** You're welcome, sir. The students are already waiting.

**PASTOR:** *(gets down from the car.)* I'm sorry. I was held in a traffic jam. *(He hands copies of seminar paper to her. She leads him to the hall where students are waiting. She distributes the papers to the students. The scene immediately changes to Pastor delivering the lecture.)* Who would try to define social vices? *(Femi raises up his hand.)* You can tell me your name and what you think it means.

**FEMI:** My name is Femi Sofole. Social Vices may be defined as problems that are caused by misbehaviour of some people in the society.

**PASTOR:** That's a very impressive attempt. Let's define it as we have it in our papers. According to this youth seminar material which tries to make it simple enough for everybody, social vice can be described as an evil or immoral behaviour or act that is considered harmful or deadly to individuals, the family, community and or to the nation directly or indirectly. The question now is: How or why vices are harmful or deadly to the nation? If you consider the number of people that had been killed or wounded physically, emotionally or spiritually, you may not really need to ask this question but for the sake of this lecture, the following can be considered as appropriate answers… *(He pauses.)*

## SCENE TWO
*(Two months, earlier Pastor is having a discussion with the Principal in his office.)*

PRINCIPAL: Pastor, we have gone through the proposal you submitted to us but we can only accept the idea of seminar on social vices with our students. The School cannot host the proposed Christian Student Fellowship, not because we don't believe in it but because it is outside of our objectives.

PASTOR: *(sighs.)* I understand your position as the Principal. So I wont address the implications of the destruction of moral values of our youths as a Pastor. I would address them as a researcher. If you give me few minutes, I can give you five reasons we have to boost the moral values of the young ones in whichever way we can. Would you be kind enough to spare the time?

PRINCIPAL: Why not? Your good intention is clear from the proposal you presented. Besides that, I know it's going to cost you a lot to reach out to all the students in this town alone.

PASTOR: Thanks for your understanding. *(He pauses for a while.)* The first reason we need a platform that will build the moral values of your students is that they can pose serious threats to many lives now and in future. If we fail to reach out and teach them the fear of God now, unscrupulous people who want to rule the country by force will destroy their moral values and then use them to cause political or civil unrest. Lenin, a Russian dictator who caused the deaths of millions of Russians said: the best revolutionists are youths devoid of morals. Edmund Burke also said that the only thing necessary for the triumph of evil is for good people to do nothing.

Secondly, if we don't build the moral values of young ones, the Government will either have to build more prisons that would accommodate the steady inflow of criminals or allow them to roam about the street, terrorizing people. Our experiences in Prison Ministry convinced us that we can reduce crimes by boosting moral values of our youths.

Thirdly, if youths are not God-fearing; the future, the politics and the economy of the nation will be in grave danger. I don't need to emphasis this point because it is quite obvious.

The fourth thing to consider is that if we have youths devoid of morals, there would be terrorism everywhere like cases of Boko Haram in the north and ritual dismemberments of human bodies in other places. If the situation is not arrested now, terrorists may bring the battles to our doorsteps.

Lastly, if we do all we can to build the moral values of young ones, we sow the good seed of love, harmony and peace which are the hallmarks of progress in every nation. *(He pauses briefly.)* I don't know if I am able to convince you enough.

**PRINCIPAL:** *(looks thoughtful.)* I think you have really made lots of valid points but, as you know, I'm not in the position to make the final decision.

**PASTOR:** You can discuss this with the School PTA members. We will abide by whatever they decide.

**PRINCIPAL:** *(nods.)* Okay.

**PASTOR:** *(brings out some tracts.)* You may have to help me distribute this among the students through their teachers. They are copies of our missionary tracts, which they can study on their own.

**PRINCIPAL:** *(takes them from him.)* Thank you, sir.

**PASTOR:** *(stands.)* Thank you too. *(He stretches his hand at him. They shake hands before he leaves.)*

## SCENE THREE

*(Miss Benson follows the Principal into his office. Both of them look upset as he takes his seat while she sits opposite him.)*

**MISS BENSON:** What are we going to do now, sir?

**PRINCIPAL:** We have no choice except to respect the decision of the PTA. That means we cannot host the Fellowship.

**MISS BENSON:** The PTA decision is wrong, sir. The reasons for not hosting the Fellowship are not reasonable at all.

**PRINCIPAL:** *(looks thoughtful.)* Yes, I know but there is nothing we can do about it. If we still go ahead and host the Fellowship, we'll put too much into jeopardy. The parents will either consider taking their students to another school or call the management to order.

**MISS BENSON:** What are you going to tell the Pastor when he comes for feedback?

**PRINCIPAL:** I don't know yet.

**MISS BENSON:** I'll like to be around when meeting him again.

**PRINCIPAL:** *(sighs.)* All right.

## SCENE FOUR

*(Miss Benson and Pastor are with the Principal in his office. There is brief silence.)*

**PRINCIPAL:** *(looks a little guilty.)* …Man of God, I don't know how to tell you this.

**PASTOR:** *(smiles at him.)* Tell me anyhow. I can read the answer through your reaction.

**PRINCIPAL:** *(bows slightly.)* Thank you, sir, for making it easy for me to tell you the outcome. We had the PTA meeting and discussed the issue as I promised. Though many of them supported the idea but a few oppose it. They said we are turning the school into…

**PASTOR:** *(interrupts.)* A Church?

**PRINCIPAL:** *(looks puzzled at him.)* How do you know?

**PASTOR:** *(smiles.)* You can never imagine how many times I have heard that in schools. What the people do not understand is the fact that no one can remain neutral in the battles of life. You either fight evils on the Lord's side or support it. By doing nothing about the evils like the social vices around us, we simply allow it spread.

**PRINCIPAL:** Yes, I pointed that to them but those who oppose the idea insisted that it is all about religion. I could not persuade them to give it a chance just as you have persuaded me. I am sorry.
**PASTOR:** *(sighs.)* You don't have to feel sorry. After all you did your best. In fact, you impress me with all your efforts.
**PRINCIPAL:** But I couldn't get you the result you expected.
**PASTOR:** The outcome doesn't matter but the efforts so far.
**PRINCIPAL:** *(brings out the tracts in his drawer.)* These are the missionary tracts you gave me.
**PASTOR:** *(takes them from him.)* Thank you very much.
**MISS BENSON:** *(looks at them.)* I have an idea, sir.
**PRINCIPAL:** What's the idea?
**MISS BENSON:** How about teaching only students from Christian homes in my class with the tracts. Christian members of the PTA never object to the idea. We can give the rest of the missionary tracts if they want it.
**PRINCIPAL:** *(looks reluctant.)* I don't know how the PTA members, especially those who kicked against it would react to that.
**PASTOR:** You should be able to defend that at the meeting.
**PRINCIPAL:** How, sir?
**MISS BENSON:** You can tell them I take the initiative to host the Fellowship in my class which is true even if they react to it.
**PRINCIPAL:** That would technically amount to insubordination. You do realize that it can cost you your job, don't you?
**MISS BENSON:** *(looks determined.)* I'll take my chances, sir.
**PASTOR:** *(looks at her.)* You don't have to risk your job for this, my sister.
**MISS BENSON:** Why not? Who cares about the job when souls are at stake? Man of God, you know Christian life is all about sacrifices because Jesus Christ makes a sacrifice of His life before we can be save. If losing a job is what can bring about salvation of others, when

can't I lose it? It'll be a light thing to do. After all, so many missionaries lost their lives while bringing the Gospel in Africa.

**PASTOR:** *(looks amazed.)* What a wonderful sister. *(He looks at Principal.)* You have to do all you can to keep this sister in the school. She is too valuable to lose.

**PRINCIPAL:** *(chuckles.)* I can't keep her if the school authority decides to do away with her. She said she is ready to face the consequences alone. If she is ready, let's stand on that.

**PASTOR:** You'll at least try and rescue her from the consequences of what she is about to do, wont you?

**PRINCIPAL:** *(shrugs.)* I can't guarantee you success.

**PASTOR:** *(looks at Miss Benson.)* I promise you in the name of the Lord that if you lose the job, God will give you another one. But I am sure you'll not lose it.

**MISS BENSON:** *(smiles.)* I believe you.

## SCENE FIVE

*(Miss Benson just finishes teaching the students, including Femi who are all getting ready for the next class.)*

**MISS BENSON:** Please, listen to this important announcement. *(Most of the students look and listen to her as she takes some tracts on the teacher's table.)* I have some tracts that can help you grow spiritually here. I want everybody to have a copy each. Secondly, we shall be having a Fellowship here every Friday immediately after school hours. *(She starts giving the tracts to the students. When she hands a copy to Femi, he shakes his head.)*

**FEMI:** I don't need it, ma. Thank you.

**MISS BENSON:** Femi, we all need it....

**FEMI:** *(looks annoyed.)* We are not Christians in my family.

**MISS BENSON:** *(smiles at him.)* It doesn't matter. It's not about religion. It's about living just and true life as in the National Anthem... Come on, you can take and read it. That's all I want from you. I'm not asking you to join the Fellowship. ***(Femi reluctantly takes the tract from her.)***

## SCENE SIX
***(Femi looks at Sola as she studies the tract, expressing disgust.)***
**SOLA:** *(glances at Femi with annoyance.)* You mean your class teacher has the guts to give you this paper in the school?
**FEMI:** Yes, mum. I told her we are not Christians in our home but she insisted that I read it. I hate her anyway. She is always trying to make me a Christian.
**SOLA:** I'll see the Principal as soon as possible. I'll inform him that he and the teacher are playing with their jobs.

## SCENE SEVEN
***(Sola sits in front of the principal in his office, looking upset.)***
**SOLA:** After we agreed at the PTA meeting that you should not introduce religion into the school, one of your teachers still has the guts to give my son this paper. ***(She throws the tract at him.)*** She didn't stop at that. She tried to make him a Christian! We are not and we don't intend to be Christians.
**PRINCIPAL:** I'm sorry, ma. I'm neither a religious person. The man who gave us the papers is trying to boost the moral values of our students. That's what the teacher is also trying to do.
**SOLA:** *(snaps.)* Whatever anyone of you tries to do, you must have respect for the religions of other people. Understood?
**PRINCIPAL:** Yes, madam. We will take note of that. ***(He is stands on his feet when Sola gets up to leave.)***

## SCENE EIGHT
***(Miss Benson stands beside her table in the classroom as David leads the rest of the students in prayers. Mary later leads the Class Fellowship in songs of praise. Later,***

*Miss Benson takes over in leading.)*
**MISS BENSON:** ...We thank God for giving us the grace to gather here again for this Fellowship. We do not need to review what we studied last week for lack of time. Let us read the memory verse in the manual together three times before we begin the study about three things we can call sin. Memory verse is found in Romans 5:12. Let's read - one - Two - Go!

**EVERYBODY IN THE CLASS:** *(reads from the paper with them.)* Wherefore, as by one man sin entered into the world, and death by sin; and so death passed upon all men, for that all have sinned... *(The students repeat the verse twice.)*

**MISS BENSON:** Good. Before we study the Bible passages that support the three things call sin, let us see what they are in the manual. One of them can be defined as violation of the word of God, according to Genesis chapter 3 verses 9 to 13. I'll explain that to you later. The second thing called sin is direct or indirect disobedience to God's specific instructions, according to Romans 3: 10-12. The third one, according to our manual is all unrighteousness and ungodliness are sins. You will find that in First John 5:17-20...

## SCENE NINE
*(Few weeks later, five boys; including Femi are with Miss Benson in the classroom.)*

**MISS BENSON:** *(frowns at Femi.)* ... Do you know that this is how secret cults begin in schools - killing birds in ritual manner?

**FEMI:** *(looks confused.)* I don't think it is an act of secret cult. We're told it is art in my father's club.

**MISS BENSON:** *(looks puzzled.)* What? This is not what you call art. This is ritual... You really mean your father takes you to the place they kill birds and dismember it?

**FEMI:** (nods.) Yes, ma.

**MISS BENSON:** Is your father a member of the club that teaches you how to perform rituals?

**FEMI:** *(nods.)* Yes, ma. But I still don't think it is ritual.

**MISS BENSON:** Any group or club that is involves in this kind of thing is actually performing rituals. And any group that demands the shedding of any type of blood is a cult. Since the children of members of your father's club are instructed how to kill chickens in such a ritual manner, the club is operating as a cult. Your father may not realize this. When you boys meet outside the school, killing birds in such a way, you are actually performing ritual sacrifices.

**VICTOR:** What is ritual sacrifice, ma?

**MISS BENSON:** Ritual sacrifice is something offered to the devil or demons in worship or adoration.

**KOLA:** *(frowns.)* We're worshiping the devil by killing birds like that?

**MISS BENSON:** That is exactly the point, my dear. Anyone who worships the devil is of the devil though he may not know it. You have to confess your sins and give your lives to Jesus if you don't want the devil to destroy your lives through cultism. Would you like to give your lives to Jesus right now? *(All the boys nod.)* You can all kneel down for prayers then. *(They kneel in front of her as she prays.)*

## SCENE TEN

*(Miss Benson comes out of the classroom with the five boys including Femi. She leads them to the Principal's office.)*

**VICTOR:** Miss Benson… *(She pauses to look at him.)* Why do you still want us to tell the Principal after we have confessed out sins to you and Jesus?

**MISS BENSON:** *(smiles at him.)* Your confession would make him realize that he did the right thing when he allowed us to set up the Class Fellowship.

**FEMI:** What if he informs our parents?

**MISS BENSON:** He may need to tell your parents for a reason.

**KOLA:** What if he decides to expel us from school?

**MISS BENSON:** I can assure you that he wont do that.

## SCENE ELEVEN

*(Miss Benson sits in front of the Principal while the boys stand beside the door in his office. He looks at them with both disbelief and annoyance.)*

**PRINCIPAL:** …Ritual sacrifice in the school? What name are you boys trying to give us in this school?

**MISS BENSON:** It is not in the school, sir. It's outside.

**PRINCIPAL:** *(looks at her sharply.)* Does that matter? They are our students. If anyone were to apportion blame to anyone, the school would be forced to take it.

**MISS BENSON:** People would know it's not the fault of the school.

**PRINCIPAL:** How? Even if we tell them, who is going to believe us? *(He looks at the boys.)* You're in for a big trouble – all of you!

**MISS BENSON:** We don't have to blame them for the mere fact that the vice started from Femi's home.

**PRINCIPAL:** *(looks at Femi.)* That's the more reason I must expel you even if I don't expel other boys. *(Femi looks sad, staring at Miss Benson.)* Yes! I have more than enough reasons to expel you. First, you're the one trying to introduce others who might have come from good homes into cultism. Secondly, your mother is among those who tried to kill the idea of the Fellowship where one of you confessed all these, besides the fact that she came here to verbally attack me for giving you the tract that can help you spiritually.

**MISS BENSON:** Sir, may I come in here? *(The Principal waves impatiently, still expressing annoyance.)* I promised the boys that none of them would be expelled from school. That's what gives them the courage to come here with me. It'll appear as if I let them down if any of them is expelled. Moreover, as I told you, it is not Femi's fault. He did not even know they are involved in ritual sacrifice, let alone to know its implications.

**PRINCIPAL:** *(looks thoughtful for a while.)* Okay. How do we stop this mess from happening again?

**MISS BENSON:** I actually brought them here to let you realize that the Fellowship you allowed me to establish in my class is a very good move. We can use this case to bring up the issue of the Fellowship up again at the PTA meeting.

**PRINCIPAL:** How are we going to do that without exposing what we are trying to cover up?

**MISS BENSON:** If you ask me, sir, I don't think we are trying to cover up anything. Presenting the case again may not need to come from you. We'll use their boys' parents, especially Femi's mother who was one of the people that opposed the idea of the Fellowship to support it.

**PRINCIPAL:** *(looks thoughtful.)* I think the idea may work if I meet the parents individually. *(He looks at the boys.)* You can tell your parents we want to see them in the school. I know how to inform them what happened. So don't tell them the reason we want to see them. *(He stares at Femi.)* I particularly want to see your mother, not your father. Okay?

**FEMI:** *(nods, a little relieved.)* Yes, sir.

## SCENE TWELVE

*(Sola is in the sitting room when Femi comes to join her.)*

**FEMI:** Mum, Principal said you need to see him in the school.

**SOLA:** *(frowns.)* Why does he want from me?

**FEMI:** *(shrugs.)* He said it is about an important issue.

**SOLA:** I see. Does it have anything to do with you?

**FEMI:** I think so.

**SOLA:** What could that be? I'll see him soon anyway.

## SCENE THIRTEEN

*(Miss Benson and Sola sit in front of the Principal while Femi stands in his office.)*

**PRINCIPAL:** Madam, I invited you here just as I have invited other parents whose children are involved in secret cult.

**SOLA:** *(looks stunned.)* What do you mean by that?

**PRINCIPAL:** You know we take the issue of academic, emotional and moral aspects of our students very seriously, which is one of the reasons I unofficially permitted Miss Benson to conduct Fellowship in her class every week after school hours. The effect of that was to have five boys confessing to her that your son influenced them to organize a club that is growing into a secret cult.

**SOLA:** *(looks impatient.)* What are you trying to tell me?

**MISS BENSON:** *(stares at Sola who sits beside her.)* When the Principal gave me the opportunity to hold the Fellowship in my class, I started using the tracts that were given to the school to reach and teach the students. A boy who later joined the Fellowship confessed what they have been doing outside the school with other boys, including your son after I taught them about sin and what it will do to them...

**SOLA:** *(interrupts her.)* What did the boy confessed?

**MISS BENSON:** He confessed that they are involved in what looks like a secret cult.

**SOLA:** You mean my son is involved in secret cultism? *(Miss Benson nods silently. Sola smiles with disbelief.)* Is that supposed to be a joke?

**PRINCIPAL:** *(raises his voice high.)* Do we sound like jokers here? *(He waves at her impatiently.)* That is where you sat when you threw the tract that was used to boost the student's moral values at me, saying all sorts of things to me! How about this for another shocker? Your husband's club, according to your son influenced him to organize the cult.

**SOLA:** *(looks amazed, staring at Femi.)* Don't tell me that's true. *(There is silence.)* Is that true? *(Femi looks sober and quiet.)* Tell me what's happening!

**FEMI:** *(in a quiet voice.)* Dad used to take me to Friends And Brothers Club where I meet other children. We're all taught how we can kill chicken in a way that looks like a... sacrifice, according to what I was told in school.

**SOLA:** *(looks at Sola and Principal with annoyance.)* Friends And Brothers Club is a social club! What gives you the impression that it operates as a cult?

**MISS BENSON:** *(in a gentle voice.)* The way your son was taught how to kill birds and remove their parts in ritual manners, calling it an Art is a very strong proof... Most secret cults pose as social clubs. Some of their members don't even know they are involved in cultism until it is too late.

**SOLA:** Oh, my God! Somebody tell me this is not happening to me! Tell me this is a nightmare!

**PRINCIPAL:** *(looks at Femi.)* Tell your mum what you have decided to do before we know how to come in.

**FEMI:** I have decided to follow Jesus Christ.

**PRINCIPAL:** *(stares at Sola who is still looking very terrified.)* Madam, there is no use lamenting over this. We need you to do two things. One of them is to tell the boy's father what he has decided to do. Both of you need to respect his decision if you don't want him to grow out of hand. Secondly, we want you to support the idea of Bible Fellowships in the school. The reason is, as the Pastor who gave us the resource materials said, if we fail to teach youths of today the fear of God, they may turn into terrorists tomorrow. We'll all face the consequences at the end. Building young ones is a collective responsibility of both parents and school teachers. If we do our jobs as teachers and some parents don't do theirs, it will affect our works. The result of that is to have other parents complaining that our school is full of bad eggs that contaminate others. We don't want that.

## SCENE FOURTEEN

*(Sola and Sofole are in the sitting room.)*

**SOLA:** Femi and other children are now Christians.

**SOFOLE:** *(in a hash voice.)* How? Why?

**SOLA:** It is because that is their decision.

**SOFOLE:** *(stands up angrily.)* I make decisions here!

**SOLA:** *(also stands up, glaring at him.)* Would you rather have our children as members of secret cults that pose as social club than to have them as Christians?

**SOFOLE:** *(frowns.)* What do you mean?

**SOLA:** The Principal in Femi's school invited me to a private meeting and inform me that he established a secret cult that meets outside the school. *(She sits.)*

**SOFOLE:** *(also sits, looking more confused.)* How?

**SOLA:** You don't want us to go into that part, do you?

**SOFOLE:** Why not?

**SOLA:** Okay... He was taught at the meetings of Friends And Brothers Club how to kill birds in a ritual manner. He tried to teach other boys in the school what he learned.

**SOFOLE:** That's not ritual.

**SOLA:** What do you call it? Art? Fun? Do you know what the school considers it to be? Introduction into cultism. *(Sofole looks sobber.)* We are going to respect their decisions. And that's final.

## SCENE FIFTEEN

*(Femi stands in front of the class, singing and clapping. The rest of the students sing with him.)*

**FEMI:** *I have decided to follow Jesus...*
*No turning back, no turning back!*
*The world behind me, the cross*
*Before me...*

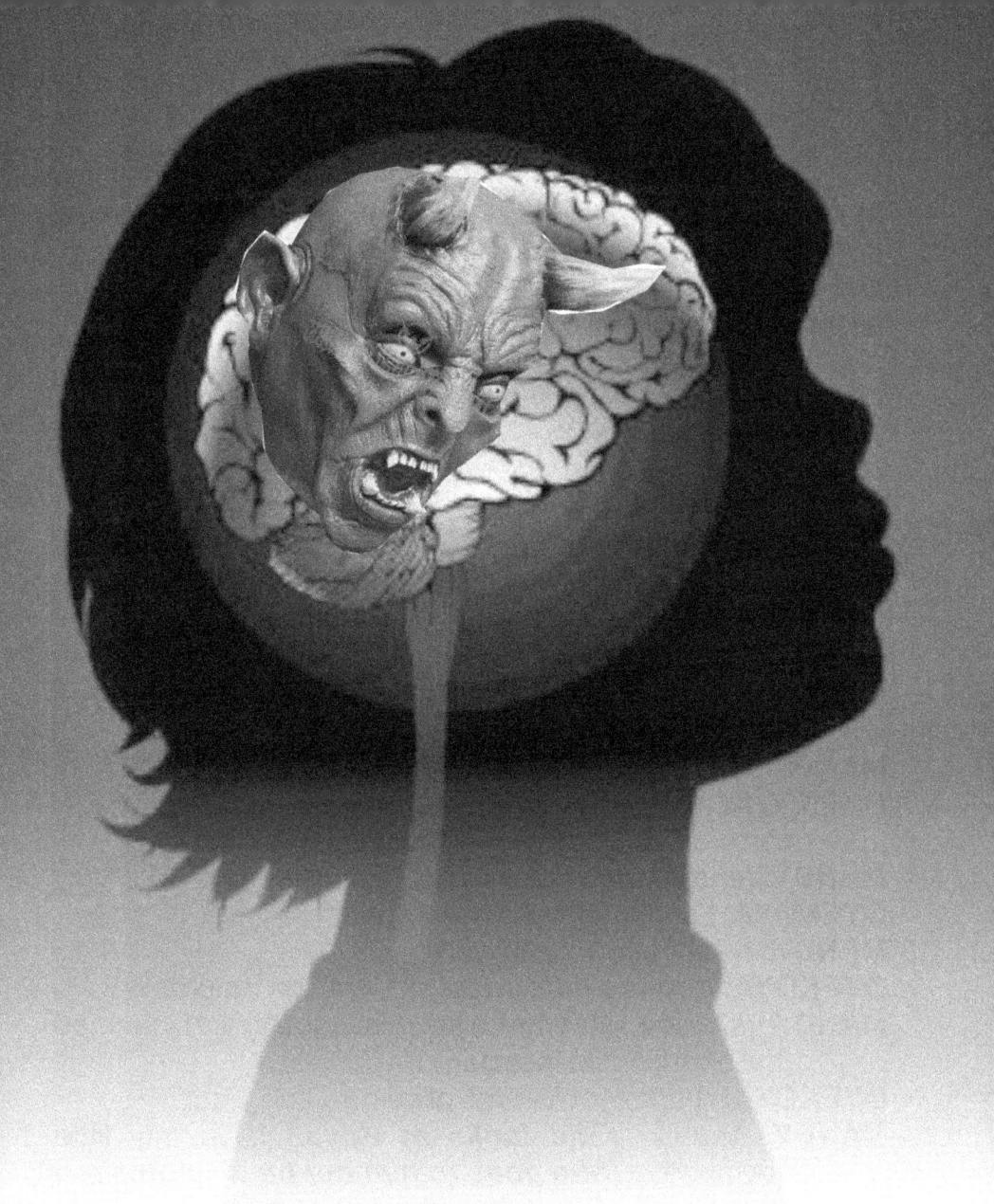

# THE BEAST IN THE CHILD

## SCENE ONE

*(Koya, a seven-year old boy is playing with toy guns and soldiers that are made of plastics as the melody of "Life Is A Very Serious Game" begins.)*

**MELODY:** *Life is a very serious game*
*Don't play with levity*
*Even though life is a challenge*
*It can make you a real champion*
*At times life can be so bitter*
*Even though it can be made so sweet…*

*(The door is knocked. After a while, Oyekoya comes out of the room and goes towards the door.)*

**OYEKOYA:** Who is it?

**MANDY:** *(from outside.)* It's Mandy…

**OYEKOYA:** Oh, Mandy… *(She opens the door.)* Good afternoon. How are you?

**MANDY:** *(in American accent.)* I'm fine. How about you?

**OYEKOYA:** I'm fine too. *(She gestures her inside.)* Please, come on in.

**MANDY:** *(enters the sitting room.)* Thanks.

**OYEKOYA:** Your husband is not around?

**MANDY:** Yeah. He's gone to work.

**OYEKOYA:** *(looks a little puzzled.)* Even on Saturdays?

**MANDY:** *(shrugs.)* He was called this morning and informed that his attention is required in the office.

**OYEKOYA:** I guess you're tired of being alone, right?

**MANDY:** Yeah…. *(She looks at Koya.)* koya, my little boyfriend… *(She goes to him but he is engrossed in the toys. She takes the toy gun from him. He looks upset.)* Hey, honey…

**OYEKOYA:** Don't mind him, Mandy. When he's playing with toys like that, he doesn't want any form of interruption.

**MANDY:** *(frowns at her.)* Do you know the implication of a boy of his age getting so engrossed in toys like that?

**OYEKOYA:** *(shrugs.)* They are meant to keep him busy.

**MANDY:** Oyekoya, don't you understand? It means something else. I'll explain it to you.

**OYEKOYA:** Before you explain anything to me, you can settle down and let me get you something to drink. *(Mandy goes to sit on a couch. She went to the kitchen.)*

## SCENE 2

*(Mandy and Oyekoya are in the sitting room with fruit drinks in front of them, sitting beside each other.)*

**MANDY:** ... As you know, I lived for almost ten years in the US. My father always insisted that I marry a Nigerian like my family. I didn't really know why until I was given a topic to research on in the College. The topic is: Causes Of Violence In The United States. The research work exposed me to a lot of materials that stunned me. I first started by reading a book titled: "Pawn In The Game", written by a researcher called William Guy Carr, born in 1895 and died in 1959. *(She shrugs.)* The guy was considered a conspiracy theorist but he seemed to have firm grip over historical facts. I was so impressed by the findings of this researcher that I memorize some parts of the book. It says, "if what I reveal surprises and shocks the readers, please, don't develop an inferiority complex because I am frank to admit that although I have worked since 1911, trying to find out why human race can't live in peace... It was in 1950 before I penetrated the secret that the wars and revolutions which scourge our lives, and chaotic conditions that prevail, are nothing more or less than the effect of the Luciferian conspiracy...

**OYEKOYA:** *(frowns.)* What does that mean?

**MANDY:** It means it was the idea of Lucifer, the falling angel that is causing a lot of bloodshed in the world, giving people reasons to go into war.

**OYEKOYA:** *(looks a little amused.)* B-but what has that got to do with the toys I gave to my son?

**MANDY:** It has a lot to do with it but I will use the case of a three year old boy I came across in the course of the research work to explain. The boy had been so brainwashed with toy guns and other weapons of violence that he did not know the difference between real ones and the toy version. One day, while his mother was at the shopping mall, the boy was told to stay with her things, including her handbag. He opened the handbag and found a gun inside. You know a lady's gun... (She gestures with her right hand.) It's a small and very handy gun. You can imagine how small it is if a boy could grip and balance it in his hands. He aimed it at his mother and pulled the trigger just as you have it with toy guns. He shot her dead!

**OYEKOYA:** *(looks stunned.)* What? Why?

**MANDY:** It's simple. The boy thought the gun was a toy. *(Oyekoya looks thoughtful.)* According to the result of my research works on the causes of violence in the United States, children are made familiar with violence through toys, computer games and movies, including cartoons.

**OYEKOYA:** This is hard to believe, Mandy.

**MANDY:** Yeah, you're telling me. But it is true. There are several cases like that. The US Police always make it look like accidents.

**OYEKOYA:** B-but… why would anyone want to create a violent society?

**MANDY:** You don't want us to go into that part, do you?

**OYEKOYA:** Come on, go ahead and tell me…

**MANDY:** Going by what I found out, it is because some elites are trying to bring about what is called the New World Order… If you Google this on the internet, you would understand what I mean…

## SCENE 3A

*(Years later, Oyekoya sits in front of Pastor as she relates the incident to him.)*

**OYEKOYA:** The woman warned me that all the toys I used to buy for my son would develop the beast in him but when she told me about some elites trying to use violence to bring about New World Order and One World Government, I snubbed it. Now the boy had grown from using toy into using real guns.

**PASTOR:** *(frowns.)* What do you mean?

**OYEKOYA:** I was cleaning the house one day… *(She looks thoughtful.)*

## SCENE 4

*(Oyekoya enters Koya's room and begins to tidy things up. After a while, she sees a gun in the corner of the room and goes to take it up, looking surprised. She slowly goes to sit down, looking more stunned as she examines it.)*

## SCENE 3B

**OYEKOYA:** … At first, I thought it was a toy gun until I discovered it was real. It took me time before I recover from the shock. I waited until I got the opportunity to ask him about the gun...

## SCENE 5

*(Oyekoya sits in the compound, looking thoughtful as eighteen-year old koya comes out of the house, looking round the compound. He sees Oyekoya, sitting alone; looking thoughtful and depressed.)*

**KOYA:** *(walks towards her.)* Mum…

**OYEKOYA:** *(looks startled.)* Koya…

**KOYA:** *(goes to sit beside her, looking concerned.)* What's wrong, Mum? You don't seem happy.

**OYEKOYA:** Yes, I'm not happy…

**KOYA:** Why?

**OYEKOYA:** I found something in your room which I didn't expect to find there.

**KOYA:** *(frowns a little.)* What is it?

**OYEKOYA:** It's a gun - a real gun.

**KOYA:** ... I'm sorry I kept it in my room.

**OYEKOYA:** Where you keep a real gun is not the issue here.

The issue is what you are doing with a gun! I … I… could have vouched that you're a good boy.
**KOYA:** *(looks annoyed.)* I'm now a bad boy because you saw the gun?
**OYEKOYA:** Do good boys keep guns?
**KOYA:** Why judging me without facts?
**OYEKOYA:** What facts would justify you keeping guns in the house? Where did you get it from and what are you doing with it?
**KOYA:** It's not mine…
**OYEKOYA:** Who owns it?
**KOYA:** It's a friend's friend…
**OYEKOYA:** *(frowns.)* What do you mean? You make friends with people who use guns. You don't mean to tell me you don't know what guns are used for, do you? Are your friends killers or armed robbers?
**KOYA:** *(looks more annoyed.)* No, mum! Why do you say that? You taught me not to attack what I don't understand. You're attacking what you don't understand!
**OYEKOYA:** *(looks very upset.)* What do you expect me to understand in the use of a gun? Now tell me what your friends do with guns?
**KOYA:** It's owned by a Security Company.
**OYEKOYA:** *(looks upset.)* I don't believe you.

## SCENE 3C

**OYEKOYA:** He did not tell me who these friends are or what they do. I don't believe anything he said about the gun owned by a Security Company… *(She falls into silence.)*
**PASTOR:** *(takes a deep breath and let it out.)* To tell you the truth, the young man could be involved in crime or he's mixing with criminals, either of which is bad enough....
**OYEKOYA:** *(looks tensed.)* Pastor, if you are right, I'm in a big trouble.
**PASTOR:** If you are in trouble, it is because you violated the

passage in Proverb 22:6, which says, ***"train up a child in the way he should go, And when his old he will not depart from it."*** From all you've been saying so far, you are the one who had been training the young man to be involved in violence...

**OYEKOYA:** *(She looks puzzled.)* How, sir?

**PASTOR:** I don't need to explain how. You already told me your neighbour told you about the impact of toy guns when your son was a child. You see, what most parents don't realize is that they train children to be experts in whatever they allow them to get involved in. If you give them toy guns instead of materials to construct houses or cars, you actually train them to be violent in future instead of inspiring them to be engineers. If you allow them to play computer games or watch movies that depict violence, you make them feel violence is normal way of life. The world is full of violence through everything we can perceive with our human senses. God does not expect us to allow our children to be familiar with anything that depicts violence. If they are, what the world experiences now is the end result. It will get worse unless something is done to curb it.

**OYEKOYA:** What am I going to do about the case of Koya?

**PASTOR:** We'll pray together now. I'll come and talk to the young man at home later.

**OYEKOYA:** Thank you very much, sir.

PASTOR: Let's pray. ***(They bow down their heads, closing their eyes as he prays.)***

## SCENE SIX

*(Pastor sits outside the house as Koya comes out with a tray of fruit drinks, walking towards him. He puts the drinks in front of Pastor on a table and goes to sit opposite him.)*

**PASTOR:** *(smiles at him.)* Thank you very much for the hospitality. God bless you.

**KOYA:** *(bows politely.)* Amen. Thank you, sir.

**PASTOR:** Actually, I know your mother is not at home. The meeting with you is arranged for only two of us. *(Koya looks curious.)* You will understand the reason as we discuss what brought me here. Let us begin the discussion by first talking to God in prayer. Let's pray. *(They close their eyes as he prays briefly. He smiles at him after the prayer.)* Do you mind if we talk about life?

**KOYA:** No, I don't mind, sir.

**PASTOR:** Before then, can you tell me how come about the possession of a real gun?

**KOYA:** *(looks offended.)* I didn't expect mum to tell you about this, sir.

**PASTOR:** Has it occurred to you that if Police traces that gun to this house, everybody; including your mum would be in a big trouble? *(There is silence as Koya looks thoughtful.)* Tell me how you're going to prove it to the Police or the people that you're not a killer? How do you expect your mum to feel seeing that kind of weapon in the house? Tell you what! The sight of that gun broke her heart into pieces. Tell me again what you expect to happen to her if you get into trouble with the Police because of that gun or if people start talking about you as a killer. You probably don't know that it is a serious case to be in possession of a gun, do you? *(He pauses, looking at his puzzled expressions.)* The problem with youths of nowadays like you is that you think you know better than adults because many parents are afraid of telling you the truth. Now tell me how you come about the gun?

**KOYA:** *(quietly.)* One of my friends told me to keep it for him. He said it belongs to one of his friends who works in a security company.

**PASTOR:** Why didn't your friend keep it instead of giving it to you?

**KOYA:** He was the one doing that until he starts sharing his room with one of his cousins who came from their hometown. He said he may see it.

**PASTOR:** Does he give you anything for keeping the gun?

**KOYA:** *(hesitates for a while.)* Yes, sir. He… em… used to give me some money for helping him to keep it.

**PASTOR:** Well, let me believe your story. If the story is true, you have to know that you have been fooled. Do you know how? *(Koya shakes his head silently, looking attentive.)* Security companies don't keep guns anywhere except in save places where people will not easily get access to them. They know that if people get access to them, they can use them for armed-robberies or murder. If these happen, they can be traced to the companies. If they trace the crimes to them, of course, the Police will pick them up as principal suspects. If supposing the gun with you had been used for armed-robbery is traced to this house, the Police would assume you're one of the robbers. *(Kola looks confused.)* If you're a suspect, your mother would be in trouble like you and I may be dragged into the case. If I'm dragged in, the Church would have to get involved as well. *(He smiles as he looks more confused.)* The reason your mother has to tell me is that this is not all about you. You have to talk to me...

**KOYA:** *(stammers.)* I… didn't know all these… I thought. it's way of making money, sir….

**PASTOR:** I know your friend must have played on your ignorance. He is either one of the people using guns for operations or they play on his own ignorance too.

**KOYA:** I don't think he's the kind of person that can use guns.

**PASTOR:** You are too young to know who is who or what a person is capable of doing. Anyway, that is not our concern here. You're our concern. Even then, I don't really blame you. Your mother confessed to me that she exposed you to toy weapons, movies and computer games that probably make you feel that violence is part of normal life... By the way, do you know drone machines?

**KOYA:** *(shakes his head.)* No, sir.

**PASTOR:** Drone machines are the kind of tools or weapons that can be controlled with remote control. They include aircraft that has no pilot inside. It can be flown to anywhere and be used to strike anyone dead through remote control. The method used is the same as what you see in computer games. *(Koya looks puzzled.)* Yes. The only difference is that one is a game while the other is real just like toy and real guns. So all along you've been playing and getting used to computer games, enjoying yourself, the devil is actually training you how to kill. You know what the Bible says about killers, including the ones that had been trained to kill. The case is the same as fornication. You don't need to sleep with a girl before you fornicate with her. People do that when they watch pornographic films or pictures. If you allow anything that is against the word of God into your subconscious mind, you open the door of your heart for the spirit that can make you do that very thing. For instance, the sight of real gun is supposed to make you feel uncomfortable but you don't feel anything about it because the toy guns and the computer games you've been playing have conditioned your mind to accept what God rejects, approve what God disapproves. This makes it easy for anyone to get involved in sins or vices or even crimes. *(He pauses for a while, looking at Koya who is sober.)* Now let's talk about life, shall we? *(Koya nods quickly.)* Life is a very serious game. No one can afford to play it with levity. Jesus said in Luke 12:15, "take heed and beware of covetousness, for one's life does not consist in the abundance of things he possesses." It means life in Jesus Christ does not consist of things of this world but things of God. If you are aware of this, you'll understand that you don't use your life anyhow as if you are not accountable for it before God. In essence, the way you use your life will determine where you will spend your eternity - hell or heaven...."

## SCENE SEVEN
*(Koya talks with Yekin, holding a nylon bag.)*

**KOYA:** I have to return this gun and the money you gave me for keeping it.

**YEKIN:** Why?

**KOYA:** My mother discovered it. It almost got me into trouble.

**YEKIN:** Why not find somewhere else to keep it and then keep the money?

**KOYA:** *(shakes his head.)* No. *(Yekin takes it from him and looks inside it.)* Yekin, what do you use the gun for?

**YEKIN:** I told you it belongs to my friends working in a security company.

**KOYA:** *(shrugs.)* Okay. But I will advise you to return it. If the Police get to know about it, you can get into trouble.

**YEKIN:** Is that what your mother told you?

**KOYA:** It doesn't matter who told me as long as it is the truth.

**YEKIN:** Did you tell her you're making money for keeping it?

**KOYA:** If that thing land you into trouble, all the money you have been making cannot get you out of it.

**YEKIN:** If I keep it very well, I don't have to border about getting into trouble.

**KOYA:** *(shrugs.)* We may see later. *(They depart to different ways.)*

## SCENE EIGHT
*(Koya addresses parents in the Church.)*

**KOYA:** … There are many things our parents need to teach us about life but the most important thing is to teach us about the fear of God and the condition of this world. If we are not taught all these things, the world will teach us the wrong things. For example, most youths like me do not know that there is a battle between the kingdom of God and kingdom of darkness over our souls. Most youths are falling victims because they do not know what they are supposed to know. There are so many weapons that are being used against us. They include means of education, information and entertainment. The word of God tells us not to kill or fornicate or commit other sins but the world makes killing of human beings appear like fun through movies and computer games. There are so many songs that encourage youths to commit suicide or get involved in crimes or sins…I didn't know I had been indoctrinated to see violence as normal life through movies and computer games until I got involved with criminals who posed as security agents. I was told to help them keep one of their guns, which they normally use to operate... I didn't know the kind of job they were involved in until they attempt to assassinate a notable political figure. They, including the boy that linked me to them were caught. I thank God once again for the life of our father in the Lord and my mother who make me realize the implication of keeping a gun. I was so naïve and stupid but that is normal for youths. I really can't say much now except to let our parents realize that your ignorance about basic things of life will affect everything about us. I want to appeal to you that you get involved in whatever interests the youths so as to educate us of the negative or positive impact in us… Thank you. **(The audience gives him a standing ovation.)**

# THE ABUSE OF YOUNG GENERATION

## SCENE ONE

*(Kujomo sits opposite Head Teacher who looks at the papers and the business card on his table as the melody of "Stop The Child Abuse" begins.)*

**MELODY:** *The abuse of children*
*Is the abuse of the future*
*Stop the child abuse!*

**HEAD TEACHER:** Mr Kujomo…

**KUJOMO:** Yes, sir.

**HEAD TEACHER:** The Director Of Studies tells me to talk to you instead of conducting the interview with you. He wants you start the teaching job in this Government school. You can tell me about the school you attended.

**KUJOMO:** *(beams at him.)* I fit thank you very good, Teacher Head. I finishes for the School For Teachers for Grade 2, 3, 4 and 5.

**HEAD TEACHER:** Wait a minute. I'm hearing this for the first. I know of Grade 2 Teachers' School. I've not heard of others.

**KUJOMO:** *(beams again.)* Oh, no… em… for the time I finish, the Government plan it…

**HEAD TEACHER:** *(looks at the papers.)* Your papers here say you graduated from College Of Education. Which one do I believe?

**KUJOMO:** You fit believe the paper, sir… The Government changing the Teachers' School to College For Education where they do for grade 3, 4 and 5.

**HEAD TEACHER:** It's okay... what does L. C. M means in Mathematics?

**KUJOMO:** It is ways people do long Arithmetic. So L. C. M mean say Long Calculate Mathematics.

**HEAD TEACHER:** *(smiles and nods.)* You pass. You can start the work tomorrow so that you go get your foolish or fool's salary this month.

**KUJOMO:** Thank you, sir!

**HEAD TEACHER:** Don't thank me. You can go and thank your godfather, Chief Rankadede who says

Government must do him the favour of giving you the job by all means.
**KUJOMO:** I go thank him! *(The melody continues as he stands up to leave the office.)*
**MELODY:** *Children are always abused*
*When they are not well educated*
*They are also abused by parents*
*If they are not taught morals*
*And if teachers don't teach them*
*right things...*

## SCENE TWO

*(Kujomo stands in front of Primary School Students, teaching them in classroom.)*
**KUJOMO:** ... I fit go Jos and come back everyday... *(He sees Musa and Saka who sit beside each other, whispering to each other's ears.)* You two boys down there! *(He points at them.)* Wetin you dey talk? *(There is silence.)* You deaf and dump? *(He goes to take cane on the table, looking angry.)* If you no tell wetin you dey talk, I go beat you so tee that you no go remember your name till you die! Stand up, you two animals! *(The boys stand up at once, looking afraid.)* Tell me your talk.
**SAKA:** *(points at Musa.)* He... Em... said you speak bad English, sir...
**MUSA:** That's not true! He was the one that said that, not me!
**SAKA:** No, I didn't. I only agreed that you speak bad English!
**KUJOMO:** *(looks very furious.)* I go kill two of you for today! Come out here! *(As the boys move forward, he grabs Musa by his shirt and begins to beat him mercilessly. While doing that Saka runs out of the classroom, moving out of the school into the street as the melody continues.)*
**MELODY:** *The vices in the society*
*Begins from the family and school*
*Vices are mothers of crimes*
*To stop crimes, stop vices*

*To stop vices, stop the child abuse*
*The abuse of children...*

## SCENE THREE

*(Ahjia treats Musa's wounds on his back in the sitting room as the melody continues. He looks as if he is trying to suppress the pains he is feeling as she treats the wound.)*

**MELODY:** *Children are often abused*
*If they are forced to do wrong things*
*Good children can often do bad*
*Through immoral things they see and hear*
*These make them parts of the vices*

**MUSA:** *(moans with pains.)* That hurts, Ahjia!

**AHJIA:** You deserve what you get for calling your teacher names.

**MUSA:** We didn't call him names, Ahjia. We only said he speaks bad English, which is true.

**AHJIA:** That's still an insult. You shouldn't have said that.

**MUSA:** Ahjia, you are taking his side. If not for my private teacher who teaches me the right thing, how would I know if the school teacher is teaching me the wrong thing?

**AHJIA:** It's okay, Musa, my son... It's okay. Forget about the teacher who is not teaching the right thing and learn from your private teacher since there is nothing we can do about him. *(She waves at his wounds.)* You can see what he did to you for being so rude to him...

## SCENE FOUR

*(Weeks later, the melody continues as Saka roams round the street in school uniform. He meets Rafiu on the way.)*

**MELODY:** *...The abuse of children...*

**SAKA:** Good afternoon, sir...

**RAFIU:** Hello. Can I help you?

**SAKA:** Yes, sir. I need your help. I'm hungry. I need some money to buy some food.

**RAFIU:** Why should I give you money? Don't you have

parents?
**SAKA:** I do but there is nothing to eat at home.
**RAFIU:** What do you mean? By the way, aren't you supposed to be in school?
**SAKA:** Yes, sir, but my teacher said he would kill me if I go to school.
**RAFIU:** Why would he do that?
**SAKA:** It's because… em..
**RAFIU:** *(interrupts him.)* Save your breath. I know you are not going to tell me the truth. I don't give my money to truants like you. ***(He walks away as the melody continues. Musa also moves away until he sees a girl hawking bread in the street.)***
**MELODY:** ***The children who are abused today***
***Will become so vicious tomorrow***
***That they will become threats to lives***
***If you abuse any of the children***
***You create hostile society…***

*(Saka grabs a loaf of bread and runs away. The girl shouts, running after him, "thief, thief!" Two men run after Saka and catch up with him, beating him until Leumas arrives in his car. He parks, gets down and hurries towards the men.)*

**LEUMAS:** Stop beating the child!
**1st MAN:** He's not a child! He's a thief!
**LEUMAS:** What did he steal?
**2nd: MAN:** He stole a loaf of bread. We'll beat him until he realizes that stealing is bad. If we don't, he may join the armed robbers that terrorize us!
**LEUMAS:** He is just a little boy. He probably stole bread because he's hungry. Besides, can't you see he's a student - the future of nation?
**1st MAN:** Well, what do you want us to do to him now? Let him go?
**LEUMAS:** You can hand him over to me. I'll report the matter to his school authority. ***(The men push Saka to him. He takes him to his car.)*** I'm taking you to your school. That's where you'll be disciplined for what you

did.
**SAKA:** Please, sir, take me anywhere but don't take me to the school.
**LEUMAS:** *(pauses by the car and stares at him.)* Why not?
**SAKA:** My teacher told me he'll kill me if I come to school.
**LEUMAS:** *(frowns.)* Why did he say that?
**SAKA:** It's because he speaks bad English and my friend and I pointed this out. I don't want him to beat me the way he beat my friend.
**LEUMAS:** Do your parents know this?
**SAKA:** No, sir. If I tell them, they will force me to go back to school.
**LEUMAS:** When did this happen?
**SAKA:** It's now... almost a month, sir. I've been staying away since then.
**LEUMAS:** Come inside the car. I'll do all I can to help you. *(They enter the car.)* Do you know why I have to help you?
**SAKA:** No, sir.
**LEUMAS:** I see you as a child who can become great in future. If you don't go back to school, you cannot become great... *(They talk on the way as he drives.)* Tell me what you'll like to become.
**SAKA:** I'll like to become the State Governor.
**LEUMAS:** If you become the State Governor, what would you do?
**SAKA:** I'll sack all the bad teachers who cannot even speak good English.
**LEUMAS:** *(laughs.)* If you want to be the Governor, you need good education.

## SCENE FIVE
*(Leumas and Saka sit in front of Commissioner who looks thoughtful in his office.)*
**LEUMAS:** ... Honourable Commissioner, this is a very serious problem. At first, I thought this boy was just exaggerating until I further investigated the matter. When I heard the teacher's spoken English, I feel

sorry for the students he's teaching. *(He waves at Saka.)* This boy has the potential to be great, going by my discussion with him but the question is: what is his chance of becoming great without quality education? *(He shakes his head sorrowfully.)* With that kind of teacher in the school, he does not stand any chance. It is little wonder that the Western world does not reckon with our certificates like the old time. Apart from that, sir, another bad effect of having such teachers in the schools is to have our children being discouraged from school as the case of this boy. When children are not encouraged to go to school, they become nuisances. From there, they graduate into rings of vices and crimes. As Edmund Burke said, the only thing necessary for the triumph of evil is for good people to do nothing. For this madness in the educational system to stop, you need to use your highly elevated office to do something, sir.

**COMMISSIONER:** *(sighs and nods thoughtfully.)* Thank you very much, Mr Leumas. You've really done this nation a great thing by going out of your way to bring this problem to my notice. If we have many patriotic citizens like you in the society, our nation will have less problems to tackle. I promise you I'll do something about this.

**LEUMAS:** Thank you very much, Honourable Commissioner.

**COMMISSIONER:** *(looks at Saka.)* As for you, I'll take you to the school myself and make sure no one hurts you. Do you understand?

**SAKA:** *(bows.)* Yes, sir.

## SCENE SIX

*(Kujomo sits in front of Head Teacher who holds a letter.)*

**HEAD TEACHER:** Mr Kujomo, the result of proficiency test which the State Government set for all public school teachers is out. You are among those who fail.

**KUJOMO:** *(looks puzzled.)* I fail? *(Head Teacher nods.)* I

talk to Chief Rankadede! He say I go pass!
**HEAD TEACHER:** You fail. *(He gives him the letter.)* Government says you can go home. You have no more job here.
**KUJOMO:** Government go give me money for house.
**HEAD TEACHER:** *(frowns a little.)* How do you expect Government to pay for if don't work? Well, you can go to Chief Rankadede and tell him that the Government have sacked you because you're too dull to teach students.
**KUJOMO:** *(takes the letter.)* This Government bad! We go bring it down! *(He stands up suddenly and leaves the office.)*

## SCENE SEVEN

*(Leumas drives his car as the melody continues. Then breaking news comes up from the radio, causing him to slam the car brake into a halt.)*
**RADIO:** … The Honourable Commissioner for education is dead in the hospital where he had been receiving treatment…

## SCENE EIGHT

*(Two months later, Ahjia sits in front of her shop as Leumas parks the car by road side, heading towards her as the melody continues.)*
**MELODY:** *… The vices in the society...*
**LEUMAS:** Good afternoon, Ahjia…
**AHJIA:** Good afternoon, Mr Leumas. It's long time since we see you around.
**LEUMAS:** It's all because of work here and there. How is the market?
**AHJIA:** We have reason to thank God though the condition in the country is critical.
**LEUMAS:** You're telling me. Anyway, do you have a pack of my usual tea?
**AHJIA:** No. I'm yet to get enough money to buy all the items I've sold.

**LEUMAS:** Why? Are there no sales?

**AHJIA:** We just agreed that the condition is critical everywhere.

**LEUMAS:** Well, God will deliver us.

**AHJIA:** Mr Leumas, do you hear of the sacked Government teachers who are clamouring for their jobs?

**LEUMAS:** Of course, I heard the news. It would be a very serious matter, Ahjia. These people want their jobs back after the death of the Commissioner Of Education.

**AHJIA:** *(looks puzzled.)* What do you mean? What has the death of the Commissioner got to do with the sacked teachers?

**LEUMAS:** It's a long story really.

**AHJIA:** Please, tell me about it. I'm very interested. Let me get you a seat. *(She gets him a chair.)*

**LEUMAS:** *(sits adjacent to her.)* Some months ago, I saw two men beating a schoolboy for stealing a loaf of bread in the street. I told them to let me hand him over to his school. The boy told me he didn't want to go back to school because the teacher would kill him for saying that he speaks bad English.

**AHJIA:** Wait a minute. Is the name of the school Mandi Local Government Primary School?

**LEUMAS:** Yes, Ahjia. You know about the case?

**AHJIA:** Yes, my son, Musa was involved in the matter.

**LEUMAS:** Really? The boy told me two of them were involved. He told me the second boy was so badly beaten that he was afraid to go back to school.

**AHJIA:** That's true. If you see the wounds all over my son's body, you will feel sorry for him.

**LEUMAS:** What did you do when your son was beaten like that?

**AHJIA:** Nothing. What would you expect ordinary citizen like me to do to the Government teacher?

**LEUMAS:** Ahjia, if we all keep thinking like that, we will compound the problem. Anyway I made some findings and discovered that the boy was telling the truth. I took him straight to the Commissioner who took action by testing the competencies of the teacher with Primary four examinations. The result was to have most of them losing their jobs. Not long after that, the Commissioner fell sick and later died!

**AHJIA:** You cannot really link the sickness and death of the Commissioner to the sacked teachers, can you?

**LEUMAS:** Not really but I have the feelings that they are related. A witch cried yesterday, a child died today. Who does not know that it is the same witch that cried that caused the death of the child?

**AHJIA:** I don't agree with that theory but I agree with you when you said we must be ready to do something about the problems in the society in our own little ways. If we don't, we only make things worse.

**LEUMAS:** That is the spirit. Those sacked teachers will continue to become parasites that are paralyzing our educational system if they are given the chance. As you know, the education sector of every society is the brain development of the nation. If there is any rot in there, it needs to be rooted out. That's supposed to be the stand as responsible members of the society.

**AHJIA:** *(nods.)* That's true...

## "I PLEDGE TO NIGERIA, MY COUNTRY"

## SCENE ONE

*(Teacher stands in front of the students as the melody of "Error Everywhere" begins.)*

**MELODY:** *There are errors everywhere*
*They can be found in the street*
*And can be found in many homes*
*They are also found in schools*
*Walking around like free people....*

**TEACHER:** ...When I was young like you, our teachers told us to make pledges to Nigeria. So we pledged to Nigeria that we would be faithful, loyal and honest. We did not know that the pledge would cage us and prevent us from doing certain things that would earn us some money in future. When I grew up, however, I discovered that the pledge does not really make sense to me. So I began to violate it. I didn't care because most if not all our leaders have violated it when they were elected or selected to rule. If you try to fulfill the pledge to Nigeria, you may not be a good business man and you may be poor for the rest of your miserable life, finding it difficult to be rich.

**DANJUMA:** But, sir, Miss Okon taught us that honesty is the best policy.

**TEACHER:** Miss Okon is not a business woman. If she is, she wont say that.

**DENJI:** Are you saying we don't have to fulfill the pledge to Nigeria, sir?

**TEACHER:** I'm not saying that really. What I'm saying is that being faithful, loyal and honest doesn't always work out for everybody.

**NGOZI:** Sir, you're supposed to encourage us to keep our promise to Nigeria, not to discourage us.

**TEACHER:** I'm not discouraging you at all. I'm only telling you what is going to work for you. What's the point of making promises you wont be able to fulfill? It doesn't make sense, does it?

## SCENE TWO A
*(kojo sits in the dark room with an interrogator, talking.)*
**KOJO:**... The teacher filled our heads with errors, destroying the system that is supposed to make us patriotic and responsible citizens of Nigeria. He made us believe that if we violate the pledge we made to Nigeria for our gain, it is okay... Since that day I began to think of how our leaders loot money in Nigeria. What also make me believe in wrong set of values the more is the kinds of music and movies I watched. I listened to songs that made me feel that vices and even violence are part of normal ways of life. Through songs and movies, I was indoctrinated and made to believe that those who know their fraudulent ways out of poverty were born to be rich without having to do any work. All they need to do is to use their heads. When I grew older, I go to parties and club houses. I heard music that negatively influenced my life...

## SCENE THREE
*(The club house is filled with youths who are dancing to the tune of Olu Maintain titled: "Yahoozee".)*

*Ewo awon boys yi*
*Kamikaze on a ketto level*
*Yahoozee!!*
*E jami si jo!*
*Yahoo oh oh*
*Yahoo oh oh*
*Yahoozee (3 times)*
*If I hammer,*
*First thing na hummer,*
*One million dollars*
*Elo lo ma je ti n ba se si naira (twice)*
*Monday, Tuesday, Wednesday,*
*Thursday boys dey hustle*
*Friday, Saturday, Sunday Gbogbo aye*
*Champagne, Hennessy, Moet for everybody,*

*Ewo, awon omoge, dem dey shake their body,*
*Everybody, enough effizy*
*Take am easy*
*It's all about Benjamins baby (Twice)*
*La la la la la la la*
*London la mule si, America la ti pawo*
*Awon oshomo gbomo tiawn*
*Awon oshomo gbomo gbin*
*To ba wunmi mole gba Tokyo lo*
*To ba wunmi ma lo Jamaica o*
*O le tun wunmi kinni mo fe lo si Germany o*
*Ki n ni mo fe lo ojo meji pere*
*Owo lo n soro o*
*If I hammer... (e.t.c)*
*Owo n be lapo mi o*
*Dide ko ba mijo ...*
*Mama charley n be lapo mi o*
*Dide ko ba mi ra*
*Dollar n be*
*Naira nbe*
*Kuruje n be*
*Paper n be*
*Lapo waaaa*
*Everything is there*
*Awon kan, awonka, awon kan..*
*Awon kan waye wa sise*
*Awon kan waye wa jaye*
*Awon kan waye wa gbowo*
*Awon kan waye ma saye*
*Awon waye wa sawo oh (Twice)*
*Yahoozee!*
*Owo n apo mi o....*

## SCENE TWO B

**KOJO:** ... All my life, I've been exposed to things that incite me against the religious; traditional and family values. I enjoyed promiscuous piece of music and things that encourage me to make money by all means. When I lost my grandmother, however, I had to attend the Church for her funeral where the Pastor preached the message about eternity and things like that…

## SCENE FOUR
*(The pastor is in front of the congregation, preaching to th people in the Church.)*

**PASTOR:** ….There are only two purposes of life. Before I tell you these purposes, let me share with you the life history of a very notorious man whose life brought about a catastrophe to mankind until he becomes a changed and famous man. The person is called Alfred Bernhard Nobel. He was born in 1833. He lived for 63 years before he died…. Yes Alfred Nobel is the famous Nobel you must have heard about through the award of Nobel Prizes to people who promote peace in the world. He was once recognized as merchant of death for inventing dynamite which was used to kill people in mass at that time. After reading a premature obituary which condemned him for profiting from the sales of arms, he diverted his fortunes to institute the Nobel Prizes. How his life was transformed is an interesting part. In 1888, the death of Alfred's brother called Ludvig caused several newspapers to publish Alfred's obituary in error. One French newspapers said about Alfred, "The Merchant Of Death Is Dead." This was one of the things that changed a notorious man into a famous person. The truth, however, is found in what William Shakespeare said. He said, "the evil that men do lives after them." So the weapon of mass destruction which Alfred Nobel invented continues to strive long after his death - even up till now, despite all his effort to stop it before he dies. *(He pauses to look round at the congregation.)* We have heard the good testimony of our dear mother, grandmother and great grandmother. She understood the purposes of life which everyone of us must understand before we can be fulfilled and before we can enjoy life to its fullness.

God did not design life to be enjoyed, especially at the expense of others. In fact, if your life is a threat to the lives of other people or their peace as in the case of Alfred Nobel, you will never get the blessing of God and you will never get the goodwill of anyone. As a matter of fact, your own life and peace would be under serious threats or attack.

Life is designed by God for the purpose of serving Him. If you study the Bible about a king called Hezekiah in Isaiah 38:1 to 5, you will understand that if you use your life to please God, He will prolong it and you will also understand reasons so many people die so young, especially in this generation. In that passage, we read that the king was sick to the point of death. Prophet Isaiah was commanded by God to go and tell him to put his house in order because he was going to die. Soon after the Prophet left, the king cried to God and reminded Him that he used his life for the purpose God designed it for. Because of that, God added fifteen years to his age. The lesson here is that a life that is used to serve God, walking with him in righteousness will be prolonged.

The second purpose life is found in the story which Jesus related to the people in Luke 12:16-20 about a rich fool. The ground of this rich man brought him so much harvest that, instead of considering how to share some with people hungry, knowing fully well that it was not by his making that he got the harvest, he said to himself, **"what should I do, since I have no room to store all my crops? I will do this: I will pull down my barns and build a greater one and there I will say to my soul, "soul, you many goods laid up for many years; take your ease; eat, drink and be happy." But God said to him, "Fool! This night your soul will be required of you; then whose will those things which you have provided? (Again, he looks round at the people.)** The lesson here is that life is designed by God for the purpose of sharing. You share your life and things with your family, needy and other people around you. It is when you use your life for the purposes it is designed for that you can enjoy it...

## SCENE TWO C

**KOJO:** ... I was really transformed when I heard this message but the society had become so corrupt that I was influenced by people and things around me. What I see everyday, including the nakedness of ladies and what I watch as movies and hear as music lured me back into my old ways of life... The case is like a fish that is caught in the river. When there is nowhere to preserve it, it goes back into the river of sins. Instead of my life to improve, I grew worst. Most of the role models, including preachers give impressionable minds like mine the wrong set of values. So I graduated from taking alcohol into taking hard drugs. I became so addicted to taking drugs that I never feel fine if I didn't take it at six hours intervals. Hard drugs are so expensive to get that I have to look for money by all means before I could get it. To get the money I need, I got involved in blood contracts. I became a hit man who kills people for money. Politicians often give me the contact to assassinate their rivals. I was also involved in kidnapping and sales of human body parts to those who use them for ritual purposes. The atrocities I have committed are much more than the kidnapping I was accused me of. We are really in the era of the evil generation that was created by the older generation who never teach us the right ways of life....

**INTERROGATOR:** If you have the chance to make one last request to anyone, what would you ask for?

**KOJO:** I only have one person to make the request to. The person is God. My request is to ask for His forgiveness even if He is not ready to give me the second chance to live in this world. I have destroyed too much of His works. What is the essence of living in the world of

evils, which I have experienced firsthand?
**INTERROGATOR:** Have you been asking God to forgive you?
**KOJO:** Yes, of course. In fact, since I've been remanded here, I've been attending the Prison Fellowship everyday. A lot of miracles have taken place in my life but the greatest of them all is salvation of my soul. I was once lost but now I'm found. I was blind but now I can see. I was on my way to hell but the Lord Jesus directed my path to heaven. I cannot ask for more. (He bursts into tears.)
**INTERROGATOR:** Let me assure you of this: God Whom you trust will not let you down. When you get out of this place, you will go and tell others the right way of life. (The interrogator disappears in the room, making Kojo to look stunned.)

## SCENE FIVE

*(Two days later, Kojo lies on the floor when the door is opened. A Police Officer enters and calls out at him.)*
**POLICE:** Kojo John!
**KOJO:** Yes, sir…. *(He gets up clumsily.)*
**POLICE:** I've been told to release you...
**KOJO:** *(frowns.)* Is it on bail, sir?
**POLICE:** No… the evidence we have pointed out that you didn't commit the crime. Some else did it.
**KOJO: (frowns.)** B-but I committed it….
**POLICE:** Yes, we know but we have no proof. *(He moves closer to him.)* Don't tell anyone you committed it otherwise you may be brought back here. I can almost see God at work here. So you go out there and lead people the right way they should go, okay?
**KOJO:** Yes, sir!
**POLICE:** Let's go. (They leave the cell.)

# ABUSED MOTHER ABUSES HER CHILD

## SCENE ONE

*(Saki who backs her child carries a block in the construction site as the melody of "The Value Of Life" begins.)*

**MELODY:** How can you know the value of life
If you do not know the weight of death?
How can you know the value of peace
If you have not gone through war?

*(Saki's child begins to cry. She puts the block down and attends to the child.)*

How can you value your well being
If you have never feel so sick?
How can you value your freedom
If you have never been a slave?
What's the value of life?
What's the weight of death...?

**BRICKLAYER:** *(comes out of the building under construction and growls at her.)* What the hell is wrong with you, young woman! If you know you can't do this work, get out of here and let someone else do it.

**SAKI:** *(in an appealing way.)* I'm... sorry... I'm trying to... to pet my child, sir... She's... em... hungry... She has not eaten anything, sir. That's the... the reason I'm working...

**BRICKLAYER:** Your child is not my concern here? My concern is the work that is lagging behind scheduled time... Anyway, it's not your fault. I told the supervisor that women don't have the strength to do this work, especially the one with a child! *(He takes his phone.)* I'll call and tell him to get me someone else. If he wants to help you and your child, he should give you money instead of telling you to do this type of job. *(As he begins to make the phone call, Saki quickly goes to kneel in front of him, pleading and crying softly.)*

**SAKI:** Please, sir, don't do this to me... I... promise you I... I'll do the job well... *(The child continues to cry.)*

**BRICKLAYER:** Please, don't see me as a mean person because I'm not. You can't do this job. If the owner of the house sees the work lagging, we'll be held responsible for it.

**SAKI:** Please, sir… g-g-give me another chance…

**BRICKLAYER:** *(takes some money out of his pocket.)* You can have this. This is all I've got with me. Go and take care of your child. *(Saki reluctantly takes the money.)*

**SAKI:** Thank you, sir. *(She stands up to pick the child up.)*

**BRICKLAYER:** Please, note that your job is done here…

**SAKI:** *(begins to cry again.)* Okay, sir…

## SCENE TWO

*(The melody continues as Saki walks down the street, still backing the child. She goes to buy a loaf of bread with a sachet of water. She gives it to the child who eats it as she walks along the road. She also eats part of the bread.)*

**MELODY:** *How do you value your condition*
*If you never experience worse condition?*
*How do you value what you have now*
*If you have never been so in need it?*

**SAKI:** *(sees and walks towards a restaurant, greeting Sarah who sits in front of the place by kneeling before her.)* Good afternoon, ma…

**SARAH:** Good afternoon. Can I help you?

**SAKI:** *(stands on her feet.)* I… em… need a job, ma… I… em… wonder if you can engage my service as an attendant or a cook, ma…

**SARAH:** I don't need anyone really. Even if we need someone, we cannot engage a nursing mother.

**SAKI:** I can do any job, ma…

**SARAH:** Don't bother yourself, trying to persuade me… (Just then Pastor comes out of the restaurant. She glances at him.) Pastor, you're through with your meal.

**PASTOR:** Yes, madam Sarah.

**SARAH:** I hope you enjoy your meal today?

**PASTOR:** Of course, I do. *(He looks at Saki.)* Hello…
**SAKI:** Good afternoon, sir….
**PASTOR:** Are you the mother of that child?
**SAKI:** Yes, sir.
**PASTOR:** *(looks a little surprised.)* How come?
**SARAH:** It's a long story, sir…
**PASTOR:** *(pauses, looking thoughtful.)* You look upset. What's the matter? Does it have to do with the child?
**SAKI:** Yes, sir. I need a job, sir, so that I can take care of the child. I… I came here to see if I can get one.
**PASTOR:** *(looks at Sarah.)* You have a job for her?
**SARAH:** Oh, no. I was trying to tell her that when you came.
**PASTOR:** *(looks at Saki again.)* Where is the father of the child?
**SAKI:** I… em don't know where he is, sir.
**PASTOR:** *(looks a little surprised again.)* At your age, you're expected to be in school instead of being a mother.
**SARAH:** Thank you, Pastor. I don't know you also see it that way. There are so many of them coming here, looking for job.
**PASTOR:** *(looks thoughtful for a while before he looks at Sarah.)* I need to talk to her. Get one of your attendants to get us two chairs over there. *(He points at the place.)*
**SARAH:** That's the problem with you, men of God. You're turning my restaurant into counseling centre.
**PASTOR:** Madam Sarah, please, do what I tell you and stop complaining.
**SARAH:** *(stands up.)* Let me arrange the chairs for you. *(She goes inside the restaurant while Pastor leads Saki to the place they will converse.)*

## SCENE THREE
*(Pastor and Saki sit opposite each other, talking.)*
**SAKI:** …. My mother dropped out of Junior Secondary School when she became pregnant of me… *(Pastor frowns a little.)* I don't even know who my father is but

I was told he is from one town in Oyo state. My mother struggled to take care of me until I was six. I had to live with my grandmother and tried to attend a school in my village.... I was able to complete my primary school at the age of fourteen before I began farm work with my grandmother. The struggle was so much that I looked for a man who would relieve me by marrying me. It was then I came across my child's father. When I became pregnant, he abandoned me .... I think it is the devil at work in my family so I accept it as my destiny.....

**PASTOR:** *(gestures at her to pause.)* Wait a minute... I don't see what the so-called devil has done here.

**SAKI:** *(looks puzzled.)* You mean you don't believe there is devil, sir? I thought you are a Pastor.

**PASTOR:** Yes, I am a Pastor and I believe there are devils, not even one but many devils. But I don't believe the real devil works that way. And I don't believe your condition is your destiny because you could have changed it. We don't call what you can change a destiny. You can still change what you call destiny now if you like.

**SAKI:** How, sir?

**PASTOR:** *(looks thoughtful for a while.)* Let me begin by saying that destiny may be something you cannot change. For instance, you didn't pick your mother or family or your country. You just find yourself there when you were born. Your present condition, however, is not a destiny but the choice you made.

**SAKI:** *(frowns a little.)* How, sir? I didn't choose this life.

PASTOR: You ignorantly chose this life just like many other youths when you were messing around with the man who impregnated you. Your mother made the same mistake. You didn't learn from it. Instead you follow her footsteps. Common sense indicates that if you choose the wrong path, you'll end up in wrong destination. Anyone that messes around with girls or boys at the time he or she is supposed to be in school is only destroying the chances of becoming successful in life.

*(He pauses briefly.)* The pains are always much more on the part of the girls who mess around with boys because they bear the burden of the children while, just like your case, the man absconds, probably looking for another stupid girl to impregnate. Have you ever asked yourself this question: for how long will you continue with this life? (He gestures at her child.) What is the future of the child if your life is like this? The irresponsible life of your mother is transferred to you. Now you're going to transfer it to this innocent child unless you do something about it. The birth of the child you're not prepared to cater for has negatively affected your life. It will also affect the nation because both of you may not contribute any meaningful thing into the society. Instead of that, you'll become liabilities or nuisances like street beggars that always seek for help.

**SAKI:** *(suddenly burst into sobs, looking at the child. She kneels down before him.)* Please, help me, sir... I don't want my child to make the same mistake and go through what I'm going through right now.

**PASTOR:** *(gestures her to sit.)* You can sit. *(She obeys.)* There is hope. You're still young. So you can still pick up from where you left off in your education.

**SAKI:** How, sir?

**PASTOR:** I'll try to get you a job so that you can take care of yourself and child and still get enough to sponsor yourself in adult or evening school. If you are more educated, you stand a better chance to get better job or do something much better for yourself and your child.

## SCENE FOUR

*(Pastor sits in front of the school proprietor, talking in his office.)*

**PASTOR:** ... As a school proprietor, I have to let you know that the nation needs your help.

**PROPRIETOR:** *(frowns.)* How, sir?

**PASTOR:** As we all know, the education sector is the part that develops the brains of the society.

**PROPRIETOR:** Yes, sir. That's true.

**PASTOR:** If this sector is defective every other sectors would be defective. The reason is that the literacy levels of the citizens in the society will determine their levels of productivity in this information age.

**PROPRIETOR:** That's correct, sir, but many people don't realize this.

**PASTOR:** You may be right. It is our duty to educate others. But that's not the point I want to make. My point is that the society will be deformed if the citizens are not informed. Not only that, the ignorance of so many people, including some so-called literates who don't appreciate this fact can make everybody fall victim of social vices. *(Proprietor nods.)* We all know that education is expensive to get for a number of reasons. Many people, therefore, cannot afford it despite all Federal and some State Governments are doing to help everybody get access to basic education. Part of the reasons lies in the ignorance of most of the people. A lot of children drop out of schools to become irresponsible parents who naturally give births to irresponsible children. This invariably increases the vices in the society. We need to woo the people, especially the youths back to schools so that they can become productive and responsible. Of course, the Governments already have more than enough students to cater for. So these youths who have missed their chances of getting free or affordable education when they had the chance would be extra burden for the Governments.

**PROPRIETOR:** *(snorts.)* If I get you right, sir, you're suggesting that private schools should provide free education for those who have missed their chances to get educated.

**PASTOR:** Well, actually... *(He pauses briefly.)*

**PROPRIETOR:** You know that is not feasible. How are we

going to meet up with the expenses of running the school if that's what you mean?

**PASTOR:** Actually, I don't mean you should run the evening or adult school for free. What I mean is that you can provide the school resources and the facilities for these youths. Out of whatever you make through the fees they can afford, you can pay the teachers who may be doing the job on part time. If you're going to charge the students anything, it would be very minimal. If you don't do this, a lot of our youths who have something to offer the society won't be able to offer it for lack of education.

**PROPRIETOR:** *(looks thoughtful for a while.)* Pastor.... I'm not sure you should be talking to the private school proprietors alone. You need to talk with the Governments too.

**PASTOR:** We're talking to the Governments. Most of them are listening. Every patriotic citizen of Nigeria has a role to play in nation building. I stand by what Edmund Burke said when he made us realize that the only thing necessary for the triumph of evils is for good people to do nothing. Similarly, the only thing necessary for the triumph of vices in our society is for patriotic citizens to do nothing. If we do nothing about the vices, the society will become so hostile that no one would be able to sleep with his two eyes closed. Let me ask you: can we afford to have that in our society?

**PROPRIETOR:** *(looks thoughtful as he shakes his head.)* No, sir... Please give me time to think about this.

**PASTOR:** I'm sorry I'm not giving you time to think about this because this is SOS call coming from Nigerian Youths who you know are our future. In fact, you need to tell other school proprietors, especially the ones in your association to do something about our future. It's a call of duty. We must not shun our responsibilities, given to us by God of creation and the nation. If you agree to start the evening or adult school now, I have your first candidate waiting outside.

**PROPRIETOR:** *(looks amused.)* Oh, what? So fast!
**PASTOR:** *(shrugs.)* Procrastination is the thief of time, the adage says.

**SCENE FIVE**

*(Months later, the melody continues as the teacher stand before the students, including Saki who are mostly youths.)*
**TEACHER:** Who can tell me what an adjective is? *(One of them raises up her hand.)*

# ENTICEMENT INTO SEX SLAVERY

## SCENE ONE A

*(Keji sits on the couch, watching the TV as melody of "Life Is All About Choices" begins.)*

**MELODY:** *Life is all about choices*
*The choice between life and death*
*The choice between light and darkness*
*The choice between good and bad*

*(After a while, there is a knock at the door. She gets up moves towards the door and pauses on the way.)*

**KEJI:** Who is it?

**YINKKA:** *(from outside.)* It's Yinka with Remi, ma!

**KEJI:** *(opens the door and smiles at the two young ladies.)* Hello, dear. *(They greet her in diverse ways.)* Come inside, please. (She leads them to the sitting room, closing the door. She gestures them to seats opposite the couch). What can I offer you, young ladies?

**REMI:** We are okay, ma. Thank you.

**KEJI:** Are you sure?

**YINKA:** Yes, ma.

**KEJI:** *(shrugs and goes to sit on the couch while the rest sit opposite her.)* I heard that both of you are planning to travel out of Nigeria.

**YINKA:** Yes, ma.

**KEJI:** What are you going there to do if I may ask?

**YINKA:** *(looks at Remi who gestures her to tell her.)* Well, ma, as we are told, we are going there to work.

**KEJI:** Were you told the kind of work you are going there to do?

**REMI:** It's... em baby sitting and...or... em... taking care of old people...

**KEJI:** Your parents were given some money, right?

**YINKA:** Yes, ma.

**KEJI:** Did you go through any form of ritual at a river or anything like that - a secret one? You were told never to tell anyone.

**YINKA:** *(exchanges glares with Remi. There is silence as*

*there is a flashback of the ritual scene.)* em....
em... technically... there is... em... nothing ...

## SCENE TWO

*(The melody continues as Priest who holds a white chicken and Nabede stands by his side at the river with Yinka and Remi who are in white wrapper, kneeling down and carrying calabash in their hands.)*
**MELODY:** *Life is all about choices*
    *The choice between peace and pains*
    *The choice between heaven and hell*
    *The choice between Christ and crisis...*
*(The Priest makes same incantations, pulls the feathers of the chicken and throws them at Yinka and Remi.)*
    *You have the power to choose*
    *You can choose between Christ or anti-Christ*
    *You can choose between life and death*
**PRIEST:** Repeat after me. I vow... *(The ladies obey.)* I will do all I am told to do... I won't betray Mr. Nabede... If I betray him in anyway... let me be struck dead... If I reveal this secret oat to anyone, let me be struck with terrible sickness....

## SCENE ONE B

**KEJI:** *(smiles at the youths.)* You don't have to tell me because I already know. *(She stands up to walk round in front of them, looking thoughtful.)* You know I once found myself in your shoes just like many other girls in this country. Out of twelve of us that went to Burkina Faso back then, three of us fell sick. We were due to fly to Europe but only the remaining nine were taken to Italy. We don't know if those other three died or survived in Burkina Faso. My guess, going by the condition we left them, they did not survive. The remaining nine of us were involved in sex hawking, pornographic modeling and bestiality.
**YINKA:** *(with Remi frowns.)* What do these words means?
**KEJI:** *(smiles and shakes her head sympathetically*

*before going to take her sit again.)* If you don't know what these words mean, it means you have no faintest idea of what you are going into. To use soft words, I would say sex hawking means prostitution. To be blunt, I would say it is sex slavery. Different kinds of men would have sex with you and give your master the money. That means you are his sex slaves. He determines the number of men that would sleep with you per day. Through that, many girls have died of Sexually Transmitted Diseases (STD) such as HIV or AIDS. *(She pauses to look at their puzzled expressions.)* Pornographic modeling is posing naked for pornographic magazines. That means people will see you sleeping around with men or animals in magazines.

**REMI:** *(looks as horrified as Yinka.)* Animals?

**KEJI:** *(nods with smiles.)* Bestiality is having sex with animals like dogs, horse or even snake.

**YINKA:** Oh, my God!

**KEJI:** That's the hideous truth, my dear. *(She pauses briefly.)* It may interest you to note that out of nine of us that made it to Italy, six died of AIDS.

**REMI:** *(exchanges glances with Yinka.)* Oh, my God!

**KEJI:** At that time, AIDS have no control. Once you are infected with HIV, it blew into AIDS which knocks the person off in no time. The remaining three of us went through hell at different places. Each of us have to sleep with at least five different men for years before we could pay off our task masters who were head bent to take all the money they have invested in our trip to Italy. Even after we became free, we became almost useless in the society except to serve men with our bodies. The Nigerian Government was informed of the human trafficking years later. We were rescued and brought back to Nigeria. I didn't know how much I have lost until I met one of my mates in a company while looking for a job.

## SCENE THREE

*(Mandy is behind her table in the office, working as the melody continues.)*

**MELODY:** *Your choices will tell whom you are*
*Your choice will determine your future*
*Your choice can determine your end*
*Your choice will determine your success....*

*(keji enters the office through the opened door, holding her hand bang and a large envelop in her hand.)*

**KEJI:** Good afternoon, ma...

**MANDY:** *(looks up from what she is working on.)* Good afternoon... Can I help you?

**KEJI:** I was told to submit my application form here, ma.

**MANDY:** *(holds out a hand.)* Let me have it. *(As she takes it from her, she frowns.)* You look familiar...

**KEJI:** You too look familiar.

**MANDY:** You are Keji?

**KEJI:** *(looks puzzled.)* Yes...

**MANDY:** *(looks excited.)* I'm Mandy! We're mates in Shawy High School!

**KEJI:** Oh, yes, Mandy!

## SCENE ONE C

**KEJI:** *(continues with her story.)* When I was reunited with my old friend, she took me to her home where I met her family. *(She looks thoughtful for a while, shakes her head before she continues.)* She told me she and some other friends envied me when they heard that I've gone to Italy but when I told her what I went through, she could not believe it...

## SCENE FOUR

*(Keji and Mandy are in the sitting with drinks in front of them.)*

**MANDY:** *(looks puzzled)* ...This is very hard to believe... Y-you mean you went to Italy empty and came back empty?

**KEJI:** If I came back with anything, why should I apply to the company as a clerk?

**MANDY:** Oh, my God! What went wrong? Many people that went overseas always have something to show for it.

**KEJI:** The truth is most don't. In fact more than half of those who bluff about making it are actually involved in illicit business. Many of them are actually in jail. Those who get deported go to other African countries because of shame. I could have done the same if not for the involvement of Government in my case. You see, there's no way you could leave the country the way I did without losing something very precious to you. *(She gestures at her.)* Take a look at you. You stay put in Nigeria while I walked into the Den of Lions, thinking I'm very fortunate to travel out of the country. You've got husband, children, good job and career… Here I am with nothing after wasting many of my productive years. *(She bursts into sobs. Mandy quickly cuddles her.)*

**MANDY:** It's okay, Keji… with God on your side, you can still recover all you have lost.

**KEJI:** God left me a long time ago on the day I entered into a covenant with those evil people.

**MANDY:** *(looks at her face.)* Do you believe God is a merciful God. *(Keji nods slowly.)* If you do, he will help you if we call on him….

## SCENE ONE D

**KEJI:** *(smiles at the youths who are attentive.)* I later discovered that my friend's elder brother owned the company. We prayed together and later introduced me to her brother who suddenly liked me. He gave me a job as his clerk. Of course, I did my best to please him. When I got the job, I began to pray to God to give me a husband. About two years after I joined the company, my boss' wife died of cancer. Can you guess who my boss later picked to replace her in his life?

**YINKA:** *(in a whisper.)* You, ma?

**KEJI:** *(in the same voice.)* Yes. *(She stands.)* That's what God can do. The valuable lesson you must learn in the story of my life is that you don't have to dine with the devil before you get something to eat. You don't have to sell your soul to get comfort. If the devil gives you a chicken, he will take a cow from you. No matter what these evil people give to you, they are going to take it back in hundred folds.

**REMI:** *(in remorseful way.)* What shall we do, ma?

**YINKA:** *(goes on her kneels. Remi does the same.)* Please, ma. We've entered into a covenant with them.

**KEJI:** Yes, I know. You've not yet entered the Den of Lions as I have done. So you still have the chance to get out of the covenant. It's a matter of changing your mind or you will become their victims. You can get up, girls. *(They stand up.)* From now on, I'll take you as my children because your mothers who told me about your plan to leave the country are my friends. So I'm going to help you and fight for you as a mother. Okay? *(Again they fall on their kneels as forms of appreciations.)* I'm taking you with me to Jos where you'll continue your education. Those people would not be able to set their eyes on you.

**YINKA:** *(with Remi.)* Thank you, ma

**KEJI:** I'll see your parents and inform them of the new plans.

## SCENE FIVE

*(The melody continues as Yinka and Remi pack their things inside the car that is packed outside the house. Keji and two women of her age group come out of the house.)*

**KEJI:** Don't forget: when those men come for their money, you can give them some of the money I gave you. Don't argue with them. Just tell them your friend is the one that take the girls away to Jos. If they still want them, let them come to me in Jos, where I can easily hand them over to the police. *(She soon enter the car with the youths who look very happy and the car* *drives away.)*

# THREE DEADLY THINGS ABOUT LIFE

## SCENE ONE A

*(The students are seated in the school hall, waiting as the melody of "I See Life" begins.)*

**MELODY:** *I see life as a serious teacher*
*Who is ready to teach the truth*
*If I were you I will learn from it*
*And get experiences I need....*

*(Speaker is ushered to the front of the youths as the melody continues.)*

*I see life as designed by God*
*Like a drama with characters*
*Everybody has a role to play*
*If I were you'll play my part....*

**SPEAKER:** Good afternoon everybody.

**THE STUDENTS:** Good afternoon, sir.

**SPEAKER:** I am sent by the State Government to talk to you about three deadly things that are killing our youths so that you can protect yourselves against all of them. This lecture is important to you, your parents, and the nation. Most people, especially youths are ignorant of these things. That is the reason they are falling victims. If you disobey the instructions that go along with this lecture, you're on your own. You cannot say you are not warned. The adage says, "to be forewarned is to be forearmed." If the Government does not arm you with the information in this lecture, you can be harmed by be the evil that had been created by evil people in our society. If you fall victims of these evils of out of your ignorance, no one - not even the Federal or the State Government can save you. I pray that the God of creation will guide and protect you. *(He pauses briefly to look round at them.)* Are you going to pay attention and follow everything I tell you?

**THE STUDENTS:** *(in diverse ways.)* Yes, sir!

**SPEAKER:** Good! Let's start now. *(He glances at the book that is opened on the podium before he* *continues.)* The first deadly thing on our list is love of money. Well before I explain this, I have to say that there is nothing wrong in making money if you go about it in a legal way and if it is not made at the expense of others. What I mean by that is this: you must not defraud or cheat others. *(He pauses again.)* If you do that, you have violated the part of the pledge we all made to Nigeria when we say we will be faithful, loyal and honest... Someone who loves money would go as far as committing crimes or even perform rituals to get it. Apart from that, love of money can make someone defraud or embezzle public fund. It can make a person diabolic enough to use fellow human beings as ritaul for money. The Bible puts it this way in 1 Timothy 6:10 that the love of money is the root of all evils. I would use the case of a young man who was determined to be rich by all means as a case for you learn from....

## SCENE TWO

*(Jinta sits with his friends, talking while they listen to him.)*

**JINTA:** ... Listen, guys! I don't believe anyone is born to be poor. If you're poor that is your problem.

**BIODUN:** You don't just become rich without doing something that will earn you some money, do you?

**JINTA:** That's exactly the point. I'm going to do something that will earn me lots of money.

**LEKE:** What are you going to do?

**JINTA:** Before I tell you, let me share with you what I discovered in the history of slave trade. The western world came to Africa and took our forefathers and mothers away to America and other parts of the western world, using them as slaves before slavery was abolished. Our fore-parents worked in those countries long before we were born. So we are born to take the wages of the work of those slaves who are our fore fathers and mothers.

**BIODUN:** How are you going to do that?
**JINTA:** It is through 419 scam! We are going to fraud the western world!

### SCENE ONE B

**SPEAKER:** ... And so this young man and so many others like that became 419 fraudsters. They began to stain the name of the country - Nigeria, making the western world to consider Nigerians as fraudulent people. If you try to apply for visas in any of the countries that consider us fraudulent, you'll have to prove that you are not a criminal.

The love of money as pointed out earlier can turn a person into criminal that would stain the name of the country. Such criminal activities always shorten the lives of Nigerian youths. If you compare the rates at which young people die in modern days with the olden days, you'll be shocked. What accounts for deaths of so many them lies in the fact that they look for money at the risk of their lives.

The second deadly thing is lust. This has to do with messing around with opposite sex like street dogs. The youths of nowadays, especially the girls make sex so cheap that boys can get it even for free. Not only that, some girls are so possessed with spirit of dog that they give away their bodies at anytime at anywhere and to anyone who asks for them. Through sex, a lot of youths have destroyed their lives. While some girls who get impregnated and after attempting to abort the pregnancy lost their lives, many of them lost their chances of getting pregnant again. Aside from that, some youths use opposite sex as ritual sacrifices for riches. I'll like to use the case of a nineteen years old girl whose mother is a school proprietress. I had the privilege to counsel this young lady about her life when I discovered that she was taking wrong step....

## SCENE THREE
*(Speaker seats outside the house, reading the newspapers as the melody continues.)*
**MELODY:** *I see life as serious game*
*Please, don't play it with levity*
*Even though life is a challenge*
*It can make you a real champion.....*

*(A car parks outside the compound. Aigboran opens the door and gets out before it drives away. She is dressed in a seductive way, walking into the compound. Speaker looks at her direction as she walks inside. The melody continues.)*

**MELODY:** *I see life as farmland*
*Where people plant their seeds*
*Whatever you plant in there*
*You will surely reap it one day....*

**SPEAKER:** Aigboran! *(She looks at his direction.)* Come here... *(She looks as if she is a little irritated, walking towards him. The melody continues.)*

**MELODY:** *I see life as a bitter pill to take*
*Take it with courage*
*Life as frustrate everything*
*Only if you give it the chance*

**SPEAKER:** Can I get you a chair to seat?

**AIGBORAN:** No, sir. **Thank you.** I'm okay like this. Besides that I've got some things to do in my room.

**SPEAKER:** Okay. *(He puts down the newspapers.)* Whatever I say now may not be pleasant to you but it is for your own good if you take it like bitter pills. No matter how harsh it sounds, you better take it as the truth. It will help you if you take it....

**AIGBONRAN:** Please, sir, say whatever you want to say and spare me all the preambles.

**SPEAKER:** *(frowns a little at her before he shrugs.)* Okay... From the last birthday you had in this compound, you are just nineteen years. Going by what the landlord told me which your uncle told him, your parents sent you to this town to study at College Of Education and then inherit your mother's school when you graduate...

**AIGBONRAN:** *(looks offended.)* Why should people poke their noses into what is none of their businesses?

**SPEAKER:** Are you addressing the question to me or your uncle or the landlord for that matter?

**AIGBORAN:** If you have any answer to the question, you can give me the reply.

**SPEAKER:** Well, I don't believe you are addressing the question to me. So I'm not going to give you any answer to it. But you have to know that if a child cuts a tree in the bush, it is the adult who knows the direction it will fall. Aigboran, I have to tell you that life is a dangerous game. You must not play it with levity.

**AIGBORAN:** Which game of life am I playing with levity?

**SPEAKER:** The life you're living is very dangerous. Life is not to be lived like that.

**AIGBORAN:** I still don't understand. How am I living any dangerous life?

**SPEAKER:** Let me explain it to you. All those boys you are dating has nothing good to offer you. They will just suck the better part of your life and throw you away like oranges that has been sucked.

**AIGBORAN:** I think I've had enough of your rantings!

**SPEAKER:** *(looks puzzled.)* You consider all I'm saying as rantings?

**AIGBORAN:** *(hisses and walks away.)* I don't know why I have to listen to you in the first place....

## SCENE ONE C

**SPEAKER:** I did not stop telling this youth the truth until the day she really insulted me and my wife....

## SCENE FOUR

*(Aigboran and speaker stand by the gate of the compound.)*

**AIGBORAN:** ... The only reason I did not react to the

nonsense you have been telling me is because you are old enough to be my father....

**SPAKER:** That's exactly the point. I see you as my daughter. If I see my daughter treading on the wrong path, it is my duty to tell her.

**AIGBORAN:** I will appreciate it if you keep your advice to yourself. I don't need it. And I don't see you as my father because you're not my father. Stop pestering my life for God's sake.

**SPEAKER:** I'm saying all these for God's sake and for your own good....

**AIGBORAN:** *(interrupts him, glaring at him.)* You have no idea how much you piss me off with your opinion of me. I said I don't need your advice.

**SPEAKER:** Oh, my God... *(He smiles at her with regrets.)* You don't need this advice?

**AIGBORAN:** *(shouts at him.)* Yes! What is your problem, old man? *(She changes her expression, nodding and smiling at him.)* I think I know your problem. You want to block my guy out of my life so that you can come in, right?

**SPEAKER:** What do you suspect I want to do with you even if I block the guy out of your life?

**AIGBORAN:** Oh, you may want occasional quick one in your bedroom when your old wife is not around.

**SPEAKER:** Must you insult me and my wife for trying to guide you on the path of real life?

**AIGBORAN:** Well, I'm sorry about that. Perhaps I will understand what you are trying to tell me if you can explain to me how you marry your wife. Didn't you date her before you married her? The guy you see with me is my fiancé.

**SPEAKER:** *(spread his hand in surrender gestures.)* I give up then.

## SCENE ONE D

**SPEAKER:** ... The adage says that the falcon that will get lost will not hear the falconer... Because I knew that she could never attract a responsible man with her kind of lifestyle, I didn't need anyone to tell me that the guy she called her fiancé was just fooling her. Even then, I didn't know that the so-called fiancé was a devil incarnate until something which no one, not even I expected happened. She suddenly fell so sick to that she was taken from one hospital to another. There was something moving round her body which no scanning machine and no doctor could detect, causing her severe stomach pains. As days rolled by, the mysterious object in her body began to grow to the point that the movement could be traced through the stomach like a baby in a womb. Her parents who sent her to school wasted all their resources until she requested to see me in her room….

## SCENE FIVE

*(Aigboran lies on the bed in the room, looking very sick as the melody continues.)*
**MELODY:** *I see life as a real document*
*Which has no duplicate*
*If you want to preserve it now*
*You need to give it to Jesus Christ*
*I see life as a battle field*
*Filled with deaths and much pains….*
*(When Speaker opens the door and silently enters the room, she begins to sob the more. Speaker quietly take a small table beside her and draws it close, sitting on it.)*
**AIGBORAN:** … I'm so sorry….
**SPEAKER:** *(in a gentle voice.)* It's okay. *(There is silence.)*
**AIGBORAN:** You're right about the guy I was dating, sir…
**SPEAKER:** Tell me what actually happened?
**AIGBORAN:** The guy turned my life into this wretch that's worth nothing…
**SPEAKER:** *(looks puzzled.)* How?
**AIGBORAN:** He is a yahoo plus guy…
**SPEAKER:** What does that mean?
**AIGBORAN:** Yahoo is a cover up name for guys who are into

cyber crimes. When it is getting difficult to make money through cyber crimes, the fraudsters adopted a diabolic method...

**SPEAKER:** What is the diabolic method?

**AIGBORAN:** It is the sacrifice of human beings to get wealth. There are many ways they do this, depending on... the instructions of the witch doctor that is consulted... Sometimes they tell the guys to get their mothers' underwear as the items that would be used. If they use the item, the blood of owner would dry up and then dies later... Sometimes they tell the guys to eat human excreta. The person who defecates the excreta would later die... Sometimes, as in my case, the guys would be given some concoctions to take and then instructed to have sex with ladies. Their semen would turn into some mysterious things that would eat up their internal organ.... That's what happened to me, sir....

**SPEAKER:** *(looks horrified.)* Oh, my God! D-did you tell your parents about this?

**AIGBORAN:** *(groans with pains.)* No, sir... If I tell them, they would be heart broken. I wouldn't tell you if not for all your efforts to warn me... Besides that, I need your prayers... I don't even have the urge to live again...

**SPEAKER:** I would definitely use your story to teach other people, especially youths like you but before we pray, I need to tell you about Jesus and what he can do for you.... *(He brings out his pocket Bible and opens it.)* I want to read what Jesus said in John 14:6. *(He begins to reads the passage.) "Jesus said to him... (He looks at her.)* As he is saying to you now... *(He reads again.) 'I am the way, the truth and the life. No one comes to the Father except through me.' (He looks up at her again.)* The three things Jesus can do for you are found in what he said. On of them is that he is the way out of all our problems, including the ones we created for ourselves and the ones by evil people we are living with in this world. Jesus is the truth, which I tried to preach to you before you fell into the hands of evil people. And lastly Jesus said he is life, which means that when we die, we will live in eternity if we are born-again. Without him, we cannot get to the Father in heaven....

### SCENE ONE E

**SPEAKER:** ... After telling her about Jesus, I prayed with her, praying for her salvation and healing. *(He pauses briefly before he continues.)* She never get healed until she died few weeks after that. *(There is silence for a while as he looks round at them. The melody continues.)*

**MELODY:** *I see life as precious people*
*Who as the power to decide*
*Where they will spend their eternity*
*If I were you I will follow Jesus...*

**SPEAKER:** The reason I have to use the real life story of this youth is that it explains all the three deadly things that are killing youths of nowadays. It is the love of money on the part of her boyfriend that caused him to use the girl as ritual sacrifice for money. It is lust that made the girl to be attracted to the guy who would cause her much pains and her death. It is pride that made the girl felt that she knew everything she need to know about life, making it difficult for me to teach her the truth about life until it was to late. Of course, it is pride that made her insulted the person who means well for her. The secrets of long life, peace and prosperity are in the truth about life. The truth about life is found in Ecclesiastes 12:13, and 14 which says, **"Let us hear the conclusion of the whole matter: fear God and keep his commandment, for this is man's all. For God will bring every work into judgment, including secret thing, whether good or evil."** *(He pauses to look round at them.)* That's all for now. Any question? *(Most of the students look sobber while some are puzzled. Only few raise up their hands to ask him some questions. He begins to take it one after the* *other, spending a little more time give to answers to their questions.)*

# AGENTS OF CORRUPTION

## SCENE ONE

*(Miss Benson teaches the student one the assembly ground, using the book: Building your success and the nation as the melody of "I did not know" begins.)*

**MELODY:** *I did not know, I did not know*
*So many things in this world*
*I did not know the world is a*
*battlefield until I see*
*bloodshed all around me*
*I did not know I am surrounded*
*by enemies until I was struck at*
*the back by a friend…*

**MISS BENSON:** *(reads from the book.)* … Success is not being wealthy or famous or in what you have achieved but rather in living a purposeful and fulfilled life. A man maybe successful as a business person and still be a failure as a married man. He may not be successful in acquiring wealth and yet a great success in other things like in the case of Florence Nightingale who came from a very rich family but sacrificed so much to serve humanity through nursing. Millionaire John Rockefeller admitted, "I have made millions, but they brought me no happiness…" *(She looks round at the students who are all attentive.)* The points in the portion in this book which everybody must note involve the fact that there are different aspects of life such as academics, careers, moral, spiritual and other aspects, including marriage. The other thing to note is that success is not limited to only one aspect. It covers everything… That is to say you successfully complete your academic programme, which started from Primary School up to Secondary School or Tertiary Institution without any malpractice. After that you begin your career as a responsible citizen of Nigerian. The moral aspect of life is very crucial because it involves you to talk to God in payers. Since we all need God in everything we do, including helping us to build our future, nobody can afford to displease Him. One of the ways people makes God angry at them is to be involved in shedding blood of fellow human beings, stealing… I don't need to tell you all the things that are wrong. Your conscience will tell you. A lot of people steal from others or the nation. Some kill in the name of politics or religions but the truth is anyone doing any of these is not on the side of God. And if you are not on the side on God, no matter the number of people on your side, God will one day strike you for getting involved in evil things. God will elevate everyone who pleases Him with his or her life... *(She pauses for a while, looking at the students.)* Shall we now take the pledge?

**THE STUDENTS:** I pledge to Nigeria, my country to be faithful, loyal….

## SCENE TWO:

*(Hope reads the book: Building your success as the melody continues.)*

**MELODY:** *I did not know what got me into trouble until I found myself begging for help*
*I did not know how much I need Jesus until I was getting close to my grave…*

*(Rajah rides a motor bike and stops nearby, parking it by the way. He gets down and goes towards her.)*

**RAJAH:** Hope…!

**HOPE:** *(looks up at him and smiles.)* Hey, Rajah. How are you doing?

**RAJAH:** I'm fine. How you?

HOPE: I'm okay...

**RAJAH:** *(looks at the book.)* Which book are you reading?

**HOPE:** It's the one we're studying in school.

**RAJAH:** *(goes to the sit close to her.)* I see. *(He smiles at her.)* How about a date this evening?

**HOPE:** My parents are around. So I can't make it. Besides that, I now have to get serious about my future.

**RAJAH:** What do you mean by that? I'm your future - your

future partner.

**HOPE:** I've come to realize that getting future partner at his age is wrong and risky.

**RAJAH:** *(looks puzzled.)* What do you mean by that?

**HOPE:** *(opens and points to the portion of the book.)* Hear what this author says here: *"the present day is important to you for this reason: you can waste it or use it, but no matter how you spend it, you've traded a day of your life for it."*

**RAJAH:** The book did not say we should not have some fun or play around. Apart from that, it is just an opinion.

**HOPE:** You don't seem to get the point.

**RAJAH:** I don't get the point.

**HOPE:** The point is I am supposed to be preparing for my future from now. What we are doing right now can damage our future.

**RAJAH:** I don't understand you again. You mean our love for each other can damage our future?

**HOPE:** Let's not pretend as if we don't know that sleeping around is wrong.

**RAJAH:** If I get your point very well, you're doing away with me. Is that it?

**HOPE:** Not really. I just want to stop jumping on the bed with you until we are married. That's going to be after I complete all my education.

**RAJAH:** *(looks thoughtful for a while.)* I see. *(He stares at her.)* You're technically asking me go around and find another love… right?

**HOPE:** No, Rajah, no...

**RAJAH:** You expect me to hang on until…

**HOPE:** What if I get pregnant or something?

**RAJAH:** We often use prevention, don't we? Please, stop giving me excuses and tell me straight away that you don't want me again. Then I'll look for another girl.

**HOPE:** *(looks thoughtful).)* I'll think about it.

**RAJAH:** I don't have that patience. Tell me the answer now.

**HOPE:** Okay, I'll… We can continue the relationship but I can't go out with you this evening.

**RAJAH:** Why?
**HOPE:** I told you my parent are around.
**RAJAH:** How about tomorrow after school?
**HOPE: (shrugs.)** Okay…
**RAJAH:** *(stands up to go.)* I'll call you on phone later. *(He waves at her.)* Love you, girl.
**HOPE:** Love you too. *(She continues reading as he goes towards his bike.)*

## SCENE THREE

*(Rajah is with his two friends Yoyo and Toye in the sitting room, chatting and smoking weed as the melody continues.)*
**MELODY:** *If I had known, I would have sold myself.*
*Yes, I would have sold myself to Jesus*
*Who pays the price of my Redemption*
*And delivers me from my enemies*
*I did not know…*

*(Rajah's phone rings. He gestures everybody to keep silence.)*
**RAJAH:** That's my baby calling… *(There is silence as he picks the call.)* Hello, Hope, sweet love… I'm fine thank you… How about our date…? *(He smiles, nodding.)* Yeah… I'm with my friends. You don't mind joining me here, do you…? Oh, no you don't have to worry about that. We'll have a room to ourselves. It's located at Johanu Estate… Once you're in the estate, I'll come and pick you up with my bike… Okay then… Love you… *(He cuts the line and beams at the rest.)*
**YOYO:** Hey, Rajah, how about sharing the girl with us?
**RAJAH:** *(looks offended.)* That's annoying. How can you ask me to share my girl with you?
**TOYE:** We did share our girls with you, didn't we?
**RAJAH:** Yes, but this girl is special to me.
**YOYO:** What do mean? You plan to marry her?
**RAJAH:** I can marry her.
**TOYE:** We all know that's a lie. Remember you said any girl you have tasted is not good for marriage with you.

**RAJAH:** I didn't say that!
**YOYO:** I was there when you said it, man!
**RAJAH:** Whether I said that or not, I can't share this girl with you, okay?
**TOYE:** Alright, let it go…
**YOYO:** No!
**TOYE:** Yoyo, come on.
**YOYO:** *(stands up.)* Come, Toye, let me tell you why you have to let her go in private.
**TOYE:** If your reason is not convincing enough, I won't let it go. *(He stands up and follows him outside.)*

## SCENE FOUR
*(Yoyo and Toye are outside the house.)*
**TOYE:** I really don't expect you to argue with him.
**YOYO:** Why not?
**TOYE:** As we normally do to the girls, we'll give the girl some drinks with the drugs that will make her grow so wild that one man wont be able to satisfy her.
**YOYO:** *(looks excited.)* We can record the fun and upload it in the playboy website.
**TOYE:** That's a good idea. That will tear them apart and prove it to him that we are not morons to share our girls with him while keeps his own away from us.

## SCENE FIVE
*(Rajah and Hope are taking fruit juice together in the sitting room.)*
**HOPE:** *(looks a little wild.)* I feel…. so… I don't know... I don't think I can wait that long before we jump into the bed...
**RAJAH:** Oh, yeah… I've arranged a room...
**HOPE:** *(gets up.)* Let's go….*(Rajah stands up, looking a little puzzled. They enter the room while Toye and Yoyo sneak into the sitting room, moving closer to the bedroom; listening to their conversation.)*
**RAJAH'S VOICE:** You don't act like this on the bed. I hope you are okay.

**HOPE'S VOICE:** I'm okay! I... just need you now... *(She moans.)* Come on... Lover boy! Let's have it... *(Toye and Toyo beam with excitement.)*

## SCENE SIX

*(Toye and Rajah are in the seating room when Rajah rushes out of the bedroom in shorts, looking angry.)*

**RAJAH:** Did you give my girl the craze drugs?

**TOYE:** *(with Yoyo exchange glances.)* What do you mean by craze drugs?

**RAJAH:** Don't pretend as if you don't know what I am talking about!

**YOYO:** Were you not the one who gave her the drinks?

**RAJAH:** I did not mix the drugs with. *(He looks thoughtful.)* Wait a minute. *(He points at Toye.)* You must have done that when I went to pick her...

**TOYE:** Accusing everyone does not solve the problem. You know what will happen if the girl is not satisfied on the bed. So let's help you out, man...

**RAJAH:** *(interrupts him.)* No! I know what is on your mind.

**YOYO:** There are only two ways out. You either go and buy the antidote at the chemist shop or we help you out.

**RAJAH:** *(smiles at them.)* You think you are smart, eh? I will take the drug as well and satisfy her on the bed. *(He looks gleeful as he leaves the sitting room.)*

**TOYE:** What are we going to do now?

**YOYO:** We'll record whatever is going on in the room and upload it on the web site.

**TOYE:** How are we going to do that?

**YOYO:** *(brings out the phone.)* I will sneak into the room and do the recording with my phone.

**TOYE:** Brilliant boy... *(Toye moves toward the bedroom.)*

## SCENE SEVEN

*(Hope sits on a bench, reading outside the house while Sade walks briskly towards her, holding a phone and a Bible. She looks worried as she walks closer to her. The melody continues.)*

**MELODY:** *I did not know…*
*Please Jesus take my life and let it be*
*I cannot live in this world without you*
*If you don't take over my life, I'm dead*
*Preserve my life till all eternity ….*

**SADE:** *(moves closer to her.)* Hope…

**HOPE:** Oh, Sade… How are you?

**SADE:** *(sits beside her.)* As you can see I'm not fine.

**HOPE:** *(frowns.)* What's wrong with you?

**SADE:** Nothing is wrong with me but a lot of things have gone wrong with your life. Take a look at this video. *(She presses some buttons on the phone and hands the phone over to her. She studies her reaction as she watches the video on the phone. Hope looks shocked.)* Is that not you acting like a street dog in the video?

**HOPE:** *(stammers.)* W-where d-did y-you get this from?

**SADE:** Someone downloaded it on the internet and send it to my phone because she knows you are my friend.

**HOPE:** Oh, my God… I'm finished… If my mother sees this… She… she would breakdown.

**SADE:** Do you have any idea about the students in our school that must have seen this? Many of them may not recognize that it's you but those who know you're the one will tell others. *(She stares hard at her.)* Why? Hope? I told you any guy you move around with does not mean any good for you, no matter how nice he tries to be and no matter the promise he makes to you… but… *(She waves indifferently.)* You'll not listen. See… see the end result. You know stuff like this does not disappear from the internet just like that. Supposing a man who proposes to marry you in future come across this stuff or someone who has the video tells him you're a cheap prostitute, would you really expect him to go ahead and marry you? Even if he does, how do you expect his family to react if they see this video? *(Hope suddenly bursts into hysterical sobs. Sade pauses for a while before she pats her* *on the shoulder.)* According to your name, there is hope for you. *(Hope dries her tears, shaking her head with sorrow.)* God says in Isaiah 1:18, *"though your sins are like scarlet, they shall be as white as snow; though they are red like crimson, they shall be as wool."* Verses 19 and 20 say, *"if you are willing and obedient, you shall eat the good of the land; but if you refuse and rebel, you shall be devoured by the sword for the mouth of the Lord has spoken it." (She looks at her and begins to explain.)* Just as I've also told you, nothing will ever be right with anyone who is not born-again. Being born-again simply means to believe in Jesus Christ, confess your sins and invite him into your life. Through that, his blood would be used to wipe out all your sins. Then you shall be as white as a snow. As John 1:12 says, if you receive Jesus into your life, you will have the right to become a child of God. If you are in Christ, according to 2 Corinthians 5:17, you are a new creation. Old things would pass away and new things would begin to take place. Then you can tell anyone who sees this video that you are not the one there. The person is dead but now alive in Christ. *(She pauses, smiling at her as she looks hopeful.)* All you need is Christ before you get over this. Would you now give your life to Christ? *(Hope nods quickly.)*

**HOPE:** You're indeed a friend...
**SADE:** No... *(She smiles when she looks puzzled.)* I'm actually your sister. *(Hope returns the smiles.)* Let's pray....

## SCENE EIGHT

*(Rajah goes towards Hope who is reading in front of the house. Hope sees him and changes her expressions into contempt.)*
**RAJAH:** *(looks jovial.)* Hi, my love...
**HOPE:** *(snorts.)* Who is your love, Rajah?
**RAJAH:** *(frowns.)* You sound angry at me. What did I do?

**HOPE:** Rajah, I'm now born-again. I gave my life to Christ the day after you messed it up by uploading on the internet the video of how you used me like a piece dirty rag.

**RAJAH:** *(looks stunned.)* That can't be!

**HOPE:** What do mean it can't be? You drug me so that I can act like a dog and you recorded all the scenes that took place in the room… *(Tears run down her eyes.)* As you can see, I'm trying to recover the shame of my past life which I believe Jesus have cleaned up. Please, don't come here and remind me of it again. Leave this place now and don't ever come back here. *(Rajah looks furious as he leaves the place.)*

## SCENE NINE

*(Toye and Yoyo are in the sitting room when Rajah enters, holding a black bag. He pulls out a small axe from the bag.)*

**TOYE:** Hey, what are you doing with that?

**RAJAH:** *(grimace with fury.)* I've come to chop off the heads of the two of you for recoding the fun I had with my girl and for uploading it on the internet.

**YOYO:** Oh, no, Rajah. Is it up to that?

**RAJAH:** *(looks insane with anger.)* Yeah, it is!

**TOYE:** You can't do that to us!

**RAJAH:** Why not?

**TOYE:** W-we are friends, remember…

**RAJAH:** What kind of friends are you? *(Rajah hit the axe on his head. Blood spills out. As Yoyo tries to escape, Rajah takes the axe and throws it at him. It hits at the back, spilling his blood. He falls down on his face. Rajah examines them and then take a knife out of the same bag and stabs himself. He falls down, dying.)*

## SCENE TEN

*(Hope stands in front of the students on the assembly ground, holding the book titled: Building Your Future And The Nation, addressing them.)*

**HOPE:** ... We are thought with this book that the people we associate with can affect a lot of things in our lives. As youths, it is easy for us to move with wrong set of people. The set of people have what it takes to destroy our potentials as leaders of tomorrow. They can turn good persons to bad people. *(She raises the book up.)* This book makes us to see that we've got our destinies in our hands. We have to protect them - protect our potentials as future good mothers and fathers - protect our potentials as future political leaders, community leaders-successful people in business and other fields and the future builders of the nation. It begins now - with what we do, what we believe and what we allow to influence us. As for me, I have made up my mind... I am not going to let anyone to destroy my life or my destiny. I know I have got what it takes to be great just like everyone here. Our greatness in life is not just our greatness but the greatness of our families, communities and nation - Nigeria. By walking towards that greatness, we are actually fulfilling the pledge we always make to our beloved county - Nigeria. Let's make the pledge once again.

**THE REST:** I pledge to Nigeria, my....

**HOPE:** *(after the recitation of the pledge to Nigeria at attention position, bows.)* Thank you. *(All the students and the teachers on the assembly ground give her a round of applause.)*

# LIFE OF DARKNESS ON CAMPUS

## SCENE ONE

*(Jeremy is dressed like a hooligan, waiting outside the classroom on campus as melody of "Save me, Lord" begins.)*

**MELODY:** *Save me, Lord, or I will die*
*Keep me, Lord, out of heat of life*
*I know I have messed up my life*
*And I have walked in my iniquities*
*I have no one to save my life…*

*(Sandra goes from one place to another, distributing tracts. She gets to Jeremy, smiles at him and hands him a tract. He takes it from her, looking indifferent.)*

**SANDRA:** How about falling in love with Jesus, my brother?

**JEREMY:** *(smiles at her.)* How about you falling in love with me, honey girl?

**SANDRA:** I really don't mind that if you fall in love with Jesus first.

**JEREMY:** *(frowns at her and shrugs after a moment.)* I'm a Christian, sister.

**SANDRA:** *(looks skeptical.)* Really?

**JEREMY:** My parents are Pastors.

**SANDRA:** *(frowns.)* That would be a little hard for me to believe. If your parents are Pastors, then we'll expect you to be a Pastor on campus. But let me ask you: are you born-again? *(There is silence.)* Forget about your parents being Pastors now and let's talk about you and God. As you must have been taught as a son of Pastors, salvation of a soul is a personal relationship between the person and God, which is brought about through acceptance of Jesus Christ as your Lord and Saviour. From that definition, do you think you are save?

**JAREMY:** *(shakes his head silently.)* No.

**SANDRA:** *(closes her eyes briefly and whispers.)* Lord, what do I do or say now? *(After a while, she looks at him again.)* What's your name, my brother?

**JEREMY:** My name is Jeremiah but I'm known as Jeremy,

The Scorpion.
**SANDRA:** *(looks puzzled.)* What? The only person I know with that name is Capo of a notorious cult on campus.
**JEREMY:** Yeah. That's me you're talking about.
**SANDRA:** *(looks more stunned.)* What?
**JEREMY:** You can still change your mind about falling in love with a cult guy. I promise you, nobody will border you.
**SANDRA:** I really don't know what to do now.
**JEREMY:** You have three options. You either fly like a bird and leave me alone or you covert me back into Christianity or you become the girlfriend of a cult guy. What's your choice, sister?
**SANDRA:** I want to covert you back into Christianity.
**JEREMY:** I know that's going to be your choice but you have to consider the risk. If you're not able to do that, you're going to be my girlfriend willy-nilly. You know what that means, don't you?
**SANDRA:** *(stares at him for a long time.)* Yes... I know what it means....
**JEREMY:** What's your decision?
**SANDRA:** I'll take my chances.
**JEREMY:** *(bursts into laughter.)* You're crazy, you know.
**SANDRA:** *(nods vigorously.)* Yeah, I know. I really want to reach out to you for Jesus...
**JEREMY:** Come on, you can't be serious. What would a decent Christian lady like you want to do with a cult guy like me.
**SANDRA:** Whether you believe it or not, I want to be your friend, at least, to remind you of what your parents must have been teaching you. You know if they get to know about your lifestyle on campus, they'll be heartbroken. They may even be discouraged in the ministries.
**JEREMY:** *(suddenly looks sober.)* I guess you're right. I'm going to need someone like you as a friend anyway....
**SANDRA:** *(brings out her handset in the bag and smiles at him.)* Give me your phone number, my friend. *(He returns the smiles at her as he dictates the number*

*to her. The melody continues.)*
**MELODY:** *The Lord is so full of compassion*
*that he will never allow me to die...*
*Though grave is ready to receive me*
*But Jesus saves me before I die...*

### SCENE TWO

*(Sandra is in her room, praying fervently as the melody continues.)*
**MELODY:** *Although I was full of atrocities*
*but I was justified by the Lord*
*All because I believe in Him*
*Then He made me his blessed child...*
*(She finishes praying and goes to take her meal which is on the table. The melody continues.)*
**MELODY:** *The Lord is so full of compassion*
*that he will never allow me to die*
*Though grave is ready to receive me*
*but Jesus saves me before I die....*
*(There is a knock at the door.)*
**SANDRA:** Who is it?
**DEBBY:** *(from outside.)* It's me, Debby…
**SANDRA:** *(sounds excited as she opens the door.)* Oh, Sister Debby… You're so welcome…
**DEBBY:** *(smiles at her.)* Thank you.
**SANDRA:** *(ushers her inside.)* Please, come on in. *(She closes the door while Debby goes to sit on the bed.)* I didn't expect to see you today. So I prepared the meal only for myself... Selfish of me, isn't it? But I can share it with you if you don't mind or, alternatively, I'll prepare another one.
**DEBBY:** Oh, come on, Sister Sandra… You're always thinking of how to please everybody. So you're not selfish. I'm okay… I actually come to tell you what the Lord revealed to me about you in a dream.
**SANDRA:** Oh, I see… *(She goes to cover the meal.)* I'm all ears, precious sister.
**DEBBY:** Take your meal first.

**SANDRA:** The meal can wait. *(She goes to sit beside her on the bed.)*

**DEBBY:** Well, it's not something so bad… I just had this revelation that God sent you to reach out to a male student on campus whom the devil had snatched from the Lord….

**SANDRA:** *(looks a little stunned.)* Wao! Actually, I just finished the three days fasting and prayers for the person.

**DEBBY:** You better keep it up with the good work because it is the Lord who sends you to deliver the man from the devil before he destroys him - completely.

**SANDRA:** *(looks thoughtful.)* Yeah… There is this burden I had for him… What initially looks like an inspiration to reach out to the brother is now an instruction from the Lord. Wao! I'm excited... *(She looks at her.)* The brother's parents must have been talking to God about him.

**DEBBY:** Really? *(Sandra nods.)* How do you know?

**SANDRA:** From what he told me, his parents are Pastors.

**DEBBY:** *(frowns.)* Oh, my God. Who is the brother anyway?

**SANDRA:** Would you believe it if I say the person is Jeremy, The Scorpion.

**DEBBY:** *(looks more stunned.)* W-what? Y-you mean the cult leader? *(Sandra nods again.)* This is not going to be a light battle, you know. To covert the Capo of a notorious cult to the side of the Lord is not going to be a joking matter at all.

**SANDRA:** Yeah? You're telling me.

**DEBBY:** But why is it that the devil always bounces on the children of servants of God and get them involved in atrocities?

**SANDRA:** I guess the answer is not farfetched. In order to get at the Christian parents who are making exploits for the Lord, the devil always seeks to use their children to destroy their ministries. It's the same old method of the devil trying to get at God for throwing him out of heaven by trying to destroy man who God so much

loves.
**DEBBY:** Yeah… *(She thoughtful and sighs heavily.)* This is a great revelation.
**SANDRA:** Yes, it is… It is from God - in His words…

## SCENE THREE

*(Few weeks later, Jeremy is in a hall with three other men when Sandra enters. Everybody looks at her direction.)*
**1ST GUY:** *(quickly goes to her.)* What do you want here, Dolly?
**SANDRA:** I'm not Dolly. *(She points at Jeremy.)* I've come to see my friend over there.
**2ST GUY:** *(glances at Jeremy before staring at her again. He and rest burst into laughter.)* The Capo is your friend?
**JEREMY:** *(looks at them and frowns a little.)* What are you doing here, Sandra?
**1ST GUY:** Is she really your friend?
**JEREMY:** Yeah, she's my friend.
**1ST GUY:** You can't be serious, Capo!
**JEREMY:** *(in a firm voice.)* Do you have problem with that, man?
**1ST GUY:** *(bows.)* I'm sorry, Capo.
**JEREMY:** *(looks at her.)* Sandra, I'm in the middle of a meeting now. So we'll have to see some other time.
**SANDRA:** *(in a firm voice.)* Do you have any idea what I went through before I find you?
**JEREMY:** But you have my number.
**SANDRA:** You're not the one picking your calls. *(She moves closer to him.)* I don't care about your meeting here. You're taking me out now! *(She looks stern. Jeremy frowns. He looks round at the rest who also express surprises.)* You're not going to deny me in the presence of your friends, are you?
**JEREMY:** *(sighs and looks at the men.)* Sandra is a stubborn bitch....
**3RD GUY:** Capo, we can't just end a crucial meeting like this because you're going on a date.

**JEREMY:** *(looks at Sandra.)* Sandra, please, you can go and wait outside. When we are done, I'll take you out. I promise.

**SANDRA:** *(hesitates for a while before she nods.)* Okay, my dear. But don't keep me waiting. *(She leaves the hall.)*

**1SR GUY:** *(points towards her direction.)* That pretty doll is not a bitch! She must be a witch! *(The rest laugh.)*

**3RD GUY:** You are damn right. Only a big time witch can bewitch a Capo Scorpion like this.

**JEREMY:** Let's get back to work, guys...

## SCENE FOUR

*(Jeremy and Sandra are seated at the Cafe, taking soft drinks as the melody continues.)*

**MELODY:** *Although I was full of atrocities*
*but I was justified by God*
*All because I believe in Christ*
*Then he made me his blessed child...*

**SANDRA:** ...I'm sorry I have to act as your girlfriend before I can get you out of that place.

**JEREMY:** You have not done anything wrong at all. In fact you really impress me with your act but... *(He chuckles.)* I know you're doing all you can to get me back to Jesus because you don't want me to reach out to you for the devil, right?

**SANDRA:** *(laughs softly.)* Somehow, you're right.

**JEREMY:** We had a deal, right? You either get me back to Jesus or you become my girlfriend. To tell you the truth, I'll say I have no reason to be at the spot you found me the first day we met... Since then, I thought a lot about you.

**SANDRA:** Hold it, brother. I hope you're not going anywhere beyond friendship. That's not the deal, is it?

**JEREMY:** What I actually want to say is that God wants to use you to bring you back to Him.

**SANDRA:** *(lets out a sigh of relief.)* I feel better now. *(He laughs.)* It shows God is already working on you.

**JEREMY:** There is more to that. With what you've done so far and with the way you acted today, I see you as an angel who is sent to deliver me from cultism....

**SANDRA:** If you really see me as an angel, you have to get out of darkness and come back to light as I've been telling you since we meet.

**JEREMY:** *(sips some of the drink.)* It's not as easy as that, you know. There is a guy who pulled out like that two years ago. The cult waited until the year he'll graduate as an engineer before they acted. His cult members killed him right in front of his parents during the graduation ceremony just to serve as a deterrent to others.

**SANDRA:** *(looks stunned.)* What?

**JEREMY:** *(nods.)* Yes. Since you've been trying to take me back to Jesus, I've been feeling restless within me.

**SANDRA:** Let's now talk about the spirit of fear as in 2 Timothy 1:7. I don't want to bring out my Bible because some of the cult guys may be around, watching me talking to you. I'm posting as your girlfriend so that the Lord can use me to get you out of the cultism.

**JEREMY:** *(nods.)* That's wisdom.

**SANDRA:** That passage tells us that God has not given us the spirit of fear but of power, and of love and of sound mind. Invariably, fear is the spirit that is opposed to the power God has given us as His children as indicated in John 1:12. It is also opposed to love of God. If not for the love of God I have for you, why should I risk mixing with a secret cult leader? But because I am not possessed with spirit of fear, I'm here trying to reach you. *(Jeremy nods thoughtfully.)* And lastly spirit of fear which obviously comes from the devil is opposed to sound mind. In other words, if you are under the influence of the spirit of fear, you won't be able to make the right decision. Fear makes you feel you will be killed if you leave the cult. But you have you to consider the fact that everybody who is involved in cultism is courting with both physical and eternal

deaths. If you consider the number of cult guys who are dead through conflicts between secret cults on this campus alone, you'll understand it is better not to come to school at all than to be a member of a cult....
*(She continues to preach to him, taking her breath and letting it out.)*
**JEREMY:** Sandra, what do you want me to do now?
**SANDRA:** I want you to leave this campus now. Going by what God reveals to me and a sister in the dream before coming to see you now, your life is in grave danger. If you have to forfeit all the years you have spent on campus, it is better.
**JEREMY:** *(looks thoughtful for a while and sighs.)* God must have truly sent you to warn me. Right now two cults, including the one I head are at loggerheads. I'm trying pacify them but they see it as a sign of weakness.
**SANDRA:** What you don't understand here is that once the spirit of bloodshed is at work, seeking to destroy, bloodshed may be inevitable. What is important is for you to run for your life when you can if you value it. Since you know this message comes from God, you will have to leave before it is too late.
**JEREMY:** *(looks more thoughtful.)* I'll leave the campus on one condition.
**SANDRA:** What's the condition?
**JEREMY:** Promise me, Sandra, that you will always be there for me. You'll not leave me...
**SANDRA:** *(frowns at him.)* I wonder what you mean by that.
**JEREMY:** *(looks rueful.)* Sandra, you're my angel, sent to me by God. As a lost child of God who is trying to find his bad ti his Father in heaven, I know what it means if an angel leaves me on my own.
**SANDRA:** *(stares at him sympathetically for a while and sighs.)* I'll try to be there for you, my brother.
**JEREMY:** *(in a quiet voice.)* Do I take that as a promise?
**SANDRA:** No, but I'll do anything the Lord wants me to do. What is important and urgent for you to do now is leave

the campus and rest for Him to sort out. I promise to keep in touch with you, praying for you...

**JEREMY:** *(smiles.)* Thank you, my... Angel. You don't mind if I call you that?

**SANDRA:** *(returns the smiles.)* No, as long as it keeps that smiles on your face.

**JEREMY:** Thanks.

**SANDRA:** I'll follow and help you pack your things if you don't mind.

**JEREMY:** Who am I to refuse the offer of an Angel?

## SCENE FIVE

*(Jeremy is at home, talking with his parents - Kayode and Morenike. They both look stunned.)*

**JEREMY:** ... Dad, I'm so sorry for the life I lived on campus... I'm a lost child but... like a prodigal son, I have come back to you...

**KAYODE:** *(looks very depressed.)* It's okay...

**MORENIKE:** *(still looks shocked.)* Y-you didn't tell us the kind of bad gang you're involved in....

**KAYODE:** *(lays his hand on hers.)* There is no need to give us details... What's important is that he comes to tell us this....

**MORENIKE:** *(looks at him with sorrow.)* The reason I'm asking is to know if we'll let him go back or not...

**KAYODE:** We'll pray about that and tell the Lord to lead us on what to do. Though we asked the Lord before we let him go to the University... I don't really know how and why it leads to this... There must be a reason why the Lord allowed this to happen... *(He sorrowfully stands up and leaves the room.)*

**MORENIKE:** *(bursts into tears.)* See how you broke your father's heart... after all his efforts... All we did... Our struggle to get you the best we can afford... We don't deserve this, you know...

**JEREMY:** *(bursts into sobs and prostrates before her.)* I'm sorry, mum... Just give me one more chance... I promise you I... I wont go back to it again... Never!

**MORENIKE:** Okay, I believe you... You can get up...
**JEREMY:** *(sits down again.)* Please, help me comfort dad... I can't stand seeing the two of you like this.
**MORENIKE:** *(smiles in the midst of her tears.)* Okay, son... I'll do that as soon as possible. I think he needs to spend time with the Lord....

## SCENE SIX

*(The sitting room is empty as the melody of "Save Me Lord" begins.)*
**MELODY:** *Save me, Lord, or I will die*
*Keep me, Lord, out of heat of life*
*I know I have messed up my life*
*And I have walked in my iniquities*
*I have no one to save my life...*
*(Kayode comes into the sitting, looking thoughtful and pacing round. After a while, he goes to sit on the couch, taking the Bible on the table. Morenike later enters the sitting room. She smiles at him when he smiles.)*
**KAYODE:** How are you feeling now, honey.
**MORENIKE:** *(goes to sit beside him.)* I feel much better. *(She puts her arms round his shoulder.)* How about you?
**KAYODE:** I think I'm fine...
**MORENIKE:** *(withdraws her hand and lean backward.)* I suppose you have decided what you want to do about Jeremiah, right?
**KAYODE:** Yes.
**MORENIKE:** What is it?
**KAYODE:** He's going to Bible College to learn to become a man of God.
**MORENIKE:** *(smiles at him.)* That's what I thought you're going to do anyway.

## SCENE SEVEN

**KAYODE:** I've prayed about all you told us about your lifestyle on campus. It's my fault...
**JEREMY:** No, dad, it's my fault... Y-you taught me all that are

required to be a good Christian. I'm the one who fail you.

**KAYODE:** It's okay, son… You may not understand what I mean… So let me take the blame... The Lord is in need of soldiers… So you're going to be one of them. You're going to Bible College...

**JEREMY:** *(looks happy.)* Praise God!

**KAYODE:** *(looks a little puzzled.)* You sound as if that's what you want.

**JEREMY:** That's what I want and that's what I pray for. I don't feel like going back to the campus.

**MORENIKE:** If that's what you wanted, why didn't you say so before your father asked you to go to the University? You would have saved us the money and the time…

**KAYODE:** There is a purpose for everything in life, honey. Besides, no knowledge is lost. Mind you, for everything we gain, we lose something and for everything we lose, we gain something. The knowledge he must have acquired on campus may come handy in the ministry of the youths.

**JEREMY:** *(looks excited.)* You're just right, Dad! Besides… I… em… met someone… *(He stops short.)*

**MORENIKE:** *(looks curious.)* Who is the person? *(There is silence.)* Now, son, tell us there is someone in your life.

**JEREMY:** *(in a quiet voice.)* Yes, mum… But I don't know if she loves me… She is the one the Lord used to bring me back to God…

**KAYODE:** Now, now, son, don't get us involved in this until you have confirmed this is what the Lord desires for you, okay? My concern now is how to get you to a reputable Bible College. *(He gets up and leaves the sitting room.)*

**MORENIKE:** *(looks at Kayode after his father leaves.)* Tell, me son, do you love this girl?

**KAYODE:** *(in a quiet voice.)* Yes, mum… But I fear she doesn't see me beyond someone that has strayed from the Lord whom she has to reach out to. She made me feel that when I return to the Lord, her job is done though she promised to be in touch with me...

**MORENIKE:** That proves she is a matured Christian...

**JEREMY:** She is. You'll like her if you see her.

**MORENIKE:** Oh, sure. I already like her, considering what the Lord has used her to do in your life. *(She looks thoughtful.)* Can you invite her here?

**JEREMY:** I don't know if she'll honour the initation but I can try...

**MORENIKE:** If you can get her here, I'll woo her for you.

**JEREMY:** *(looks excited.)* Really? *(She nods with smiles.)* How?

**MORENIKE:** You can leave that to me. I know how to handle a descent girl like her.

## SCENE EIGHT

*(Debby is with Sandra in the room. Debby looks excited as she converses with her.)*

**DEBBY:** ...You need to tell your friend what happened to all the cult members that were involved in the conflict three days ago.

**SANDRA:** He must have heard the news. Even if he hasn't, I'm sure one of his friends on campus must have informed him.

**DEBBY:** What if nobody tells him?

**SANDRA:** *(shrugs.)* If he calls, I'll tell him. I don't have time to call him except he calls...

**DEBBY:** I expect you to be excited at this. It is a great testimony, isn't? You know if he had not listened to what God told him through you, chances are that he might be dead by now.

**SANDRA:** Yeah, you're right.

**DEBBY:** Considering the role you played as his girlfriend and stuff like that, you're truly his Angel; aren't you?

**SANDRA:** Sister Debby, that is what is actually making me to stay clear of him. I don't want to play any role any more.

**DEBBY:** *(studies her face closely.)* Are you sure you are

not afraid of something?
**SANDRA:** *(frowns at her.)* What do you assume I'm afraid of?
**DEBBY:** You're afraid of what may come up between two of you, aren't you?
**SANDRA:** *(frowns the more.)* Of course not! What are you talking about?
**DEBBY:** *(jeers at her.)* Hello, we are talking about Brother Jeremiah! You tell me what's on you mind... I'm your sister and friend. You better tell me the truth... *(There is silence.)* Are you sure you are not hiding something from me?
**SANDRA:** *(sighs.)* Okay... Sister Debby, stop acting like a witch who knows too many things...
**DEBBY:** *(giggles for a long time.)* Ahaa, somebody is about to make a confession. Come on, tell me what's going on in your mind. If I can't help you, I can at least advise and pray with you.
**SANDRA:** *(nods and whispers.)* Yes, I know... You're the only one I can trust with this. First of all, I have to say you're the heroine in what happened to Brother Jeremiah. When all these started, I did not really know what I was doing until you shared your revelation with me....
**DEBBY:** My sister, you know Jesus is the hero here, not me and not even you. What I'm anxious to know is your feelings for this brother. I can sense love when I see one.
**SANDRA:** You may be right. *(She sighs again.)* At first, I thought the feeling was a burden to pray for him and that's all until the day I told you he called me his Angel. When he said he was a lost child of God... I felt so much pity - so much... call it love if you like. I couldn't it... When I offered to help him pack his things when leaving the campus, he treated me like... a queen. Things really became complicated that day... I couldn't help thinking of him, you know... *(She pauses, looking thoughtful.)* He called and told me

last week that he would like to invite me to meet his mother…

**DEBBY:** *(looks excited.)* Wao! That's amazing. He went that far? *(She nods silently.)* Why didn't you tell me all these before now?

**SANDRA:** I was actually thinking about it... But things are getting more and more complicated as I could not keep my mind off him.

**DEBBY:** *(nods with understanding, looking thoughtful.)* This is a serious matter... It's obvious both of you are in love. God must have allowed that for the purpose of… Now don't tell you don't know that.

**SANDRA:** To tell you the truth, I don't know what's happening to me. I'm confused.

**DEBBY:** I may be able to explain it better to you if you tell me other things he told you. I mean how come his mother getting involved in this?

**SANDRA:** *(looks thoughtful again.)* Whatever your thoughts may be, you may be right. He said he told his parents a lot about me after he did what I told him to do. He said his mother has lots of respect for my maturity in Christ and she wants to see me and thank me... Bla... bla... bla...

**DEBBY:** You mean you consider what he said as bleating?

**SANDRA:** I'm sorry if that's what it means.

**DEBBY:** How did you reply him?

**SANDRA:** *(shrugs.)* I told him there was no need to thank me but I'll think about the invitation.

**DEBBY:** That's not a bad reply really. At least, you didn't outrightly turn him down.

**SANDRA:** He told me something that almost made me change my mind about thinking about anything.

**DEBBY:** What is it?

**SANDRA:** *(shrugs.)* He said he'll ask his mother to make the request if I snub the invitation.

**DEBBY:** *(frowns.)* He said that to you?

**SANDRA:** Yes.

**DEBBY:** How did you respond?

**SANDRA:** I didn't say anything because I didn't know what to say. I just repeated what I told him and cut the line.
**DEBBY:** Oh, don't you think that's a bit rude to do that?
**SANDRA:** *(looks puzzled.)* Really? Well, I'm sorry.
**DEBBY:** He may not really see it that way. What I feel you should have done is to let his mother invites because… You want to know my thoughts now… His mother may become your mother- in-law! *(She laughs at her.)* My friend would get married soon.

## SCENE NINE

*(Jeremy is in the sitting room, talking on the phone.)*
**JEREMY:** …Sandra… you really mean the cult guys eventually went into war…? *(Morenike comes inside.)* Oh, my God… I know many of them will die… *(He looks at her.) Hold on a minute, Sandra...*
**MORENIKE:** *(in a quiet voice.)* I heard you calling her name…. Can I speak with her?
**JEREMY:** Sandra… em … my mother is here… She wants to speak with you… *(He chuckles.)* I didn't go to her… She heard me calling your name…
**MORENIKE:** *(frowns at him.)* She doesn't want to talk to me?
**JEREMY:** Oh not that… mum. She accused me getting her into trouble by inviting you into the discussion...
**MORENIKE:** *(smiles.)* Oh, I see… *(She stretches her hand at him.)* Let me have the phone if she does not object to my speaking with her… *(He gives her the phone.)* Hello, Sandra, my dear… *(She pauses and laughs.)* Oh no, my daughter, he didn't eventually get you into trouble… I just want to thank you so much for the part you have played in bringing back our prodigal son. God bless you… You sound so modest and well trained from Christian home… You're welcome… I told Jeremiah to invite you down here for dinner… Yes, he told me you said you'll think about it… What's your response now…? If it's going to take that long, can we come and visit you in the school then? I'm eager to see

you... Okay then, if you don't want us to come to you, you'll have to find time to come here soonest... Okay, thank you for honouring the invitation... God bless you... You can speak to him... Bye... *(She hands the phone back to him and leaves the room while Jeremy continues the conversation on phone.)*

## SCENE TEN

*(Sandra packs a few things in her bag while Debby sits on the chair.)*

**DEBBY:** You better prepare to stay there for at least a day because your mother-in-law-to-be may insist that you stay that long.

**SANDRA:** You sound as if I'm already in courtship with Jeremiah.

**DEBBY:** That's the truth, going by what we've been talking about. You just don't want to accept it. You're going to be a Pastor's wife. That's great, isn't?

**SANDRA:** *(appears ready to move.)* Let's go. *(As they leave the room, she looks at her.)* You'll do me some good if we talk about something else.

**DEBBY:** *(shrugs.)* Okay...

## SCENE ELEVEN

*(Sandra and Jeremy sit together on the couch with drinks in front of them, talking.)*

**SANDRA:** ... By the way, when is your mum coming back?

**JEREMY:** She would be back soon. She didn't expect you'll arrive here so soon. She actually went out to do some shopping because of you.

**SANDRA:** *(looks a little stunned.)* What? Are you serious?

**JEREMY:** *(smiles and nods.)* Yes. That's to tell you how important you are to her.

**SANDRA:** Now tell me what you've been telling her that makes her feel I'm so important?

**JEREMY:** *(in a quiet voice.)* Sandra, I'm not good at pretending or hiding things. Apart from telling her how God used you to save my life on campus, I told her how much I love and respect you. *(She pretends to look puzzled.)* Now don't tell me you don't know I love you, do you?

**SANDRA:** We do have an agreement.

**JEREMY:** *(looks thoughtful for a while.)* I'm not sure I know what the agreement is.

**SANDRA:** We agreed that we are not going beyond friendship, didn't we?

**JEREMY:** Well, I don't remember having that agreement with you. Even if we have, events have taken over that. You know why? *(She shakes her head slowly.)* Well, my father told me that he knew the Lord made me go to the University for a purpose. It may be different from our purposes but there is a purpose for being on campus. I believe the purpose is you. If you don't agree to become my wife, that purpose may be defeated… *(There is long silence.)*

**SANDRA:** *(looks thoughtful for a while.)* What other things convinced you that we are meant for each other? Did the Lord reveal that to you?

**JEREMY:** *(reluctantly nods.)* I think so…

**SANDRA:** You think so? You're not even sure. This is an issue of marriage, not a trivial matter, you know.

**JEREMY:** Sandra, I… I don't want to lie to you… but the truth is: there are many ways God reveals His will to his people… My mother is convinced…

**SANDRA:** Your mother? I'm not going to marry your mother, am I?

JEREMY: Oh sure, you are!

**SANDRA:** *(chuckles.)* Are you serious?

**JEREMY:** Yes, I'm serious. She used to say that anyone who would marry any of her children would also need to marry her.

**SANDRA:** Now that's the issue we really have to trash out now...

**JEREMY:** What she actually means by that is that she'll hand me over to your parents as their son while she takes you as her daughter. Exchange is no robbery, she used to say.

**SANDRA:** *(laughs.)* Your mum must be a wonderful mother.

**JEREMY:** She is… *(The door opens and Morenike comes in, carrying three polythene bags with her. The two of them are startled.)*

**MORENIKE:** I hope I didn't disturb your meeting, did I?

**JEREMY:** *(with Sandra stands up.)* Oh, no, mum…

**MORENIKE:** *(smiles at Sandra.)* That's the princess I've anxious to meet, right?

**SANDRA:** Welcome, ma. *(She goes to kneel briefly before her and takes two of the bags.)* I'm… not a princess… but I'm your baby girl.

**MORENIKE:** My baby girl, it is! *(Jeremy takes the third bag from her.)* No, that bag is meant for my baby girl…

**SANDRA:** *(looks a little puzzled.)* Me? *(Jeremy shrugs and exchanges the bag with the two bags with her.)*

**MORENIKE:** *(smiles at her.)* Yes… I've been shopping all day, trying to get the best I can afford for baby girl. *(She looks at Jeremy.)* Take these ones to the kitchen. They full of kitchen stuffs...

**SANDRA:** Wait, let me take them there… *(She puts the only bag with her on the centre table and goes to take the two with Jeremy. She whispers into his ear.)* I think I'll marry your mother instead of you. *(He bursts into joyful laughter.)*

**MORENIKE:** *(looks curious.)* Would someone share the joke with me?

**JEREMY:** She said…

**SANDRA:** Hold it. I'll say it myself. Before you come, Jeremiah told me anyone who is going to marry any of your children must be married to you. He told me what that means. When you buy me things… I could not help telling him that I'll like to marry you instead of him.

**MORENIKE:** *(laughs.)* Gracious God! I can't when last I feel so happy… Come, Sandra, let's go and cook in the kitchen. I can do with your sense of humour.

**JEREMY:** How about me?

**MORENIKE:** You stay where you are. After all she came here because I invited her…

**JEREMY:** *(shrugs.)* Okay. *(He goes to sit down on the couch while the ladies go to the kitchen.)*

## SCENE TWELVE

*(The melody continues as there is a wedding between Jeremy and Sandra in the Church two years later.)*

**MELODY:** *Although I was full of atrocities*
*but I was justified by the Lord*
*all because I believe in him*
*Then he made me his blessed child…*
*Keep me, Lord, out of heat of life*
*I know I have messed up my life*
*And I have walked in my iniquities*
*I have no one to save my life…*

# HARVEST OF BAD SEED

## SCENE ONE

*(The melody of "Harvest Of Bad Seed" begins as Governor talks to someone on the phone.)*

**MELODY:** *No one knows when the bad seed was planted
but everyone can see the bad harvest
Many have planted wrong seed in children
but they are yet to see the bad harvest
Leaders plant bad seed inside children
If they do not invest into their lives
Parents also destroy the future
if they refuse to train up their children...*

*(Funmi comes inside the office, holding a file as the melody continues.)*

*Teachers who take advantage of students
may be forced to pay back when it is time....*

*(Governor looks at Funmi as he puts down the phone.)*

**FUNMI:** This is the file you asked for, Your Excellency.

**GOVERNOR:** *(takes it from her, opens it and glance through the papers inside.)* Okay, you can go.

**FUNMI:** Your Excellency, the Executives of the Association Of Pensioners you gave an appointment two weeks ago are waiting to see you.

**GOVERNOR:** *(without looking away from the file.)* You can reschedule the meeting for next week

**FUNMI:** *(hesitates for a while.)* Your Excellency, they are em ... elderly people...

**GOVERNOR:** *(looks briefly at her, hesitating for a while.)* You want me to attend to them now because they are elderly people?

**FUNMI:** That's what they requested, Your Excellency...

**GOVERNOR:** Do you know that one of the people was my teacher in Junior Secondary School?

**FUNMI:** *(looks a little puzzled.)* I... don't know that, Your Excellency... Even then, I think that should be one of the reasons you may need to put their requests into considerations.

**GOVERNOR:** On the contrary, that is the reason I want to

reschedule the appointment and postpone the time I'll meet their request till - perhaps the time I leave office *(He laughs when she looks puzzled.)* I'm just joking.

**FUNMI:** You must have been offended by the person, Your Excellency.

**GOVERNOR:** Yes, I am…

**FUNMI:** Your Excellency, I think you may put the rest of the pensioners into deep considerations.

**GOVERNOR:** Yes, that's the reason I'm giving them my attention in the first place… *(He looks thoughtful again.)* Okay, let them to come in after thirty minutes. By then, I would be done with this file.

**FUNMI:** Yes, Your Excellency. Thank you for the considerations. *(She leaves the office)*

## SCENE TWO

*(Funmi comes out of the inner office to her own office while the melody continues as the elderly men looks at her expectantly.)*

**MELODY:** *What people in the position of influence sows inside children determines the future....*

**MORRIS:** *(moves closer to Funmi.)* Did you deliver our message?

**FUNMI:** Yes, baba. He told me to tell you to come back the next week. *(He exchanges glances with the rest of the two.)* But I told him you had a valid appointment with him today. He is aware of that but because you're elderly people… He told me to give him thirty minutes before I let you in.

**MORRIS:** What if other more important visitors come and engage him before then. That was what happened the last time we came here.

**FUNMI:** Baba, pray that that does not happen. Under these circumstances, that is the best I can do.

**MORRIS:** Okay, thank you, my daughter. God will bless you.

## SCENE THREE

*(The three elderly men sit in front of Governor who looks*

*thoughtful for a while.)*
**GOVERNOR:** ... You've come to complain that the Government owns you six months pension, right?
**MORRIS:** *(bows.)* Yes, Your Excellency.
**GOVERNOR:** So who are you blaming for that?
**MORRIS:** We are not blaming anyone, Your Excellency, we've only come to appeal to you to put us into consideration. We understand that the Federal Government budget is yet to be passed.
**GOVERNOR:** If there is anyone to be put into consideration, it is the workers.
**MORRIS:** Your Excellency, does that mean we cannot get our pension so soon?
**GOVERNOR:** I cannot guarantee you'll get it so soon. There are debts to clear.
**KOLA:** *(in a quiet voice.)* Your Excellency, we served this State with the productive part of our lives and... a lot of our colleagues are dying because of lack of money to take care of themselves....
**MIKE:** The pension is the only means of our survival, Your Excellency...
**GOVERNOR:** Are you blaming me for that? *(He looks at Morris.)* Mr. Morris ...
**MORRIS:** *(frowns like the rest.)* Your Excellency, you know my name?
**GOVERNOR:** *(smiles.)* Yes, I recognize you very. How can I forget you? You were a teacher in Denili Secondary School, isn't it. *(The elderly men exchange glance.)*
**MORRIS:** Yes, Your Excellency... I don't recall meeting you...
**GOVERNOR:** *(stands up to stretch himself. The men attempt to stand up as well.)* No, have your seats, please. I just want to stretch myself. I have been sitting for over six hours no stop. *(He paces around as he converse with them.)* I was one of your students. *(The rest look more puzzled. He smiles at them.)* Yes, I was your student. *(He gestures at Morris.)* You had the chance to make positive influence in us back then but instead you took advantage of us and

extracted as much money as you could money from our parents. Our parents were always forced to pay for most of the things the Government has paid for back then. The teachers always divided the money among themselves instead of putting it into the Government purse as they claimed. Technically, you could say all along you were extorting students back then, you were taking your pensions.... *(He becomes silent, looking thoughtful.)*

**KOLA:** B-but... Your Excellency... *(Governor raises up his hand. He stops short.)*

**GOVERNOR:** I know you're going to ask me about other good teachers .... *(He goes to take his seat again.)* I'll put them into considerations... But for now, there's nothing I can do ...

## SCENE FOUR

*(Morris stands in front of some people in the hall who are seated, listening to him.)*

**MORRIS:** ... If there is anything wrong with the society, we - the teachers and the parents who are in the position to influence young minds are the cause. The Governor made some points when we had meeting with him in respect of our pensions. These points made me realize that I was one of the people that made him develop unpatriotic attitude. When he told us the story which I remembered vividly, I felt so guilty and ashamed of myself that I could no longer say a word. It was glaring that I was not in the position to represent the pensioners again. I have to tell you this story so that everybody would understand that our responsibilities to this nation through the young ones in our care are much. *(He pauses to take his breath.)* About twenty-five years ago, I was a teacher in Denli Secondary School where the Governor began his education. The Governor was one of my pupils....

## SCENE FIVE

*(Young Morris stands in front of the students in class reading a textbook to them.)*

**MORRIS:** Mr. Danjuma is a trader. He has a shop down the street… *(He looks at the pupils, some with textbooks and some without.)* How many of you have bought this textbook? *(Most of the students raise up their hands.)* Those of you who are yet to buy it should come out. *(Some of them came out. He points outside.)* Go into the sun and stay there. That's where you'll be until we finish the class. *(The students, including Remen stay outside as the melody of "Harvest Of Bad Seed" begins.)*

**MELODY:** *No one knows when the bad seed was planted....*

## SCENE SIX

*(Morris, Remen and his father - Sambo - are with Head Teacher in his office. All except Remen are sitting, facing the Head teacher.)*

**HEAD TEACHER:** *(looks at Sambo.)* You have no reason to complain about what was done to your son since he doesn't have the textbook.

**SAMBO:** Excuse me, sir. Even if there is anything to buy in school, the parents are to buy it, not their children. So if there is anyone you should punish for not buying the textbook, the parents are to be held responsible, not the children.

**MORRIS:** We cant do anything to parents. That is the reason we dealt with your boy and other students. We know if we punish them, parents will respond.

**SAMBO:** That's against justice and moral ethics. I am telling you what you did is not right. In any case, the Government makes us to understand that our children are to be given free education and that includes giving them textbooks.

**MORRIS:** *(flies into rage.)* What's wrong with you, people?

You expect Government to do everything for you. Government should get food for you, cook for it for you and serve it for you without any contribution on your part? Government should also provide everything your children needs as well - everything Government!

**SAMBO:** Please, teacher, don't misunderstand me. We are made to believe Government have provided the textbooks. If for any reason that is not true, that does not mean you should punish the pupils. By punishing them for what is not their fault, you are making them to grow hostile against the society or discouraging them from school for that matter...

## SCENE SIX

**MORRIS**:... The boy's father was forced to pay for all what the Government had paid for. Of course, no one knew the boy had grown hostile against the teachers and no one knew he was going to be a Governor. According to the boy which is now the Governor of the State, he has a dialogue with his friends which proved that whatever our leaders had become, parents and teachers are responsible....

## SCENE SEVEN

*(Remen and other students are on the field, sitting down and chatting.)*

**REMEN:** ...Why do we have to pay for everything in school when the Government said they are giving us free education?

**CHUCKS:** I think the teachers are the ones taking the money from our parents. That's what my father said.

**LEKAN:** *(looks angry.)* Don't we have someone to report them to the Government?

**FEMI:** Who is going to report them?

**REMEN:** My father said he would have reported them but they will find a way to punish me for it. You should have seen the hard work he did before he could pay what they asked us to pay in school.

**LEKAN:** When I grow up I will look for way to torture the teachers.
**REMEN:** My father told me to struggle hard to become somebody in life. Then I'll be in the position to punish those who are using their power anyhow....

### SCENE FOUR C

**MORRIS:**.... The Governor said what we did to him and what his father said to him made him to lack consideration for others since no one put him into consideration when he was young. That is why he could divert the pensions of the elderly people to another project... but while having the meeting with the Governor we made him realize something important...

### SCENE THREE B

*(Governor stares indifferently at Morris as he speaks politely with him.)*

**MORRIS:** .... Your Excellency, I must admit that I am not in the position to say anything again, having said all these.... I am very sorry for all I have done that almost affected your life. Please, accept my apology....
**GOVERNOR:** I accept your apology but the fund for the pension have been used for a very crucial project. So you'll have to wait until the State receives its next allocation.
**MORRIS:** You already said that, Your Excellency. I just want to say this.... We want you to consider our colleagues who served the State Government faithfully. I am ready to face the consequences of my unfaithfulness and failure to fulfill the pledge I made to Nigeria but many of our colleagues we have come to represent were faithful when they were in service..... they are dying, Your Excellency. They don't deserve what I deserve....

### SCENE FOUR D

**MORRIS:** ... It was after we appealed to his emotions that he decided to pay our pensions at once. In fact, he was so impressed that he not only paid all the arrears of our pensions, he also congratulated me for the courage to admit my unfaithfulness and dishonesty. I want you to note that the students in your care may not know some things that are wrong within the system now but when they grow up and realize those wrong things, they may want to seek revenge just as in my case. The bottom line is: whatsoever seeds we sow in the minds of young ones shall be reaped one day - wether good or bad.

# THE WALKING DEAD

## SCENE ONE A
*(The melody of "Hope Is Never For The dead" begins with Kremi lying on the bench, looking as if he is in pain. Moses sits close to him, looking unhappy.)*
**MELODY:** *Hope is never for the dead*
*But for those who are alive*
*Hope is the source of human well being*
*So do not lose the hope you have....*
**MOSES:** ... Uncle, how did this happen to you?
**KREMI:** *(looks uncomfortable.)* It is a long story... Moses... I will tell you... so that you can learn from.... from my mistake... For a long time I messed... around with all kinds of women even though my mother - your grandmother told me it is a dangerous way of life.....

## SCENE TWO
*(Kremi comes out of the bedroom with Oroki just as Mama enters the sitting room.)*
**MAMA:** *(in a harsh voice.)* Kremi! Who is this one again?
**KREMI:** Please, Mama, don't embarrass me! She is my woman....
**MAMA:** *(interrupts him.)* Your woman? How many women are you going to bring into this house?
**KREMI:** Mama, please, let me live my life as I want. If you are not satisfied, you can go back to the village.... *(He looks at Oroki and pulls her.)* Please, let's go.... *(Mama goes to sit down dejectedly while the two lovers leave the room, going outside. He looks at Oroki who looks upset.)* What's wrong, my dear?
**OROKi:** Your mother sounds as if you are a playboy. Is that what you are?
**KEMI:** Don't mind the old woman. I am her last child and she is treating me as if I am still a baby....

## SCENE THREE
*(Mama is still in the sitting room, looking unhappy as the melody continues.)*

**MELODY:** *Even when the cloud seems so dark*
*never lose hope come what may*
*Think of the special ability you have*
*When things seem so gloomed hopeless*

*(Kemi enters the sitting room and sees Mama, looking sad. He walks to her.)*

**KREMI:** What is wrong now, Mama?

**MAMA:** Life is not meant to be lived the way you are living it. Anyone who chooses your kind of lifestyle is living in danger!

**KREMI:** What kind of danger?

**MAMA:** I wish you understand what I am trying to tell you. You see, human beings are dangerous. Apart from that, changing women or men like cloths instead of setting down in marriage can attract evils.

**KREMI:** Evils like what?

**MAMA:** Let me put it this way. Your father died while sleeping around with women, including the married ones.

**KREMI:** Okay, Mama, I will be careful. I wont mess around with married women.

**MAMA:** *(looks frustrated.)* This is a serious matter!

**KREMI:** *(stands up.)* Okay, I wont mess around with any woman…

**MAMA:** Where are you going now?

**KREMI:** *(pauses and looks at her.)* What again.

**MAMA:** I want you to settle down with a woman.

**KREMI:** Okay, I will. Can I go now...?

## SCENE ONE B

**KREMI:** … I did not listen to your grandmother…… Instead I went further into the lifestyle of a.... dog. I met a Christian lady called Ngozi one day….

## SCENE FOUR

*(Kremi drives a car while Ngozi walks along the road, holding a Bible as the melody continues.)*

**MELODY:** *Think of the unspeakable treasure in you*
*though may not seem no matter to you*

*Think of how to gather the piece of your life even if you are scattered in the inside…..*

**KREMI:** *(packs the car beside Ngozi.)* Hello, sweetie!

**NGOZI:** *(looks at him, frowns a little and then brightens up again.)* Hello, my brother.

**KREMI:** Where are you going?

**NGOZI:** I am going to the Church over there. *(She points at the direction.)*

**KREMI:** Can I take you there?

**NGOZI:** It is not far, sir. Thank you.

**KREMI:** Can we go to the Church together then? Who knows if I'm going be converted by you?

**NGOZI:** *(smiles and shrugs.)* Okay…. Lets go... *(She enters the car. Kremi drives away as the melody continues.)*

**MELODY:** *Think of what you can achieve with your life instead of thinking of what you have lost*
*Think of the life in eternity in the midst of everything in this world*
*Think of what Jesus has done for you instead of what you can enjoy in the world....*

## SCENE ONE C

**KREMI:** ... I took Ngozi to the Church where she preached to me about Jesus. I pretended to be moved by her sermon because I wanted to make her my girlfriend…

## SCENE FIVE

*(Ngozi and Kremi sit in the Church, talking.)*

**NGOZI:** *(holds her Bible as she preaches to him.)* ... According to the passage in the Bible in 1Timothy 5:6, *"he who lives in pleasure is dead while he lives..."* There are so many things that can cause the death of anyone who is not born again. The enemy of mankind whom we all know as the devil or Satan can use anything to fight us. He uses our flesh to fight us. He uses money and other things to fight us. That is the reason the Bible says in the book of 1 John 2:15-16 says .... *(She begin to read the Bible.)* *"Do not love the world or the things of the world. If anyone loves the world, the love of the father is not in him. For all that is in the world - the lust of flesh, the lust of the eyes and the pride of life - is not of the father but is of the world..."*

## SCENE ONE D

**Kremi**: ... I pretended to be born again that day... I told her she could be coming to take me to the Church every Sunday. She was happy but she didn't know what I was planning to do to her until one Sunday when she came to take me to the Church....

## SCENE SIX

*(Ngozi waits in the sitting room, holding the Bible while the melody continues. After a while, there is a scream in the room.)*

**NGOZI:** *(looks frantic.)* Brother Kremi, what is wrong?

**KREMI:** *(shouts in the room.)* Help! Help! Someone help me! *(Ngozi drops the Bible and hurries inside the room. As soon as she enters the room, he closes the door and locks it, smiling at her. She looks shocked.)*

**NGOZI:** W-what are y-you t-trying t-to do?

**KREMI**: Ngozi, you know how much I love you....

**NGOZI:** *(looks puzzled.)* And so what?

**KREMI**: Let's play game of love...

**NGOZI:** *(frowns at him.)* What do you mean?

**KREMI:** Come on, don't pretend as if you don't understand what I'm talking about.

**NGOZI:** Brother Kremi, what's the meaning of all these? If you don't want me to scream at you, you better open this door and let me go now!

**KREMI:** You can't scream because you came into my room so that we can have a quick one, isn't it?

**NGOZI:** Brother kremi, if you must know this, I will tell you I'm a virgin and I have vowed to God that I will remain a virgin until I get married. If you rape me for trying to help you to find the Lord, there would be grave consequence.

**KREMI:** *(looks determined.)* I'll take my chances. *(He bounces on her and pushes her to the bed and begins to struggle with her, using pillow to cover her mouth.)*

## SCENE ONE E

**KREMI:** ...I raped Ngozi that day...
**MOSES:** *(looks shocked.)* What?
**KREMI:** *(He begins to groan with more pains.)* I took her virginity and she cried....

## SCENE SEVEN

*(Kremi sits beside Ngozi who is sobbing in the bedroom.)*
**NGOZI:** Why did you do this to me…?
**KREMI:** I'm sorry, Ngozi… I love you…. I want to marry you...
**NGOZI:** This is not love…. What you did to me shows how much you hate me. I was seeking for your salvation and growth in Christ. See what you did to pay me back. You took my virginity, my virtue and spoil my testimony….
**KREMI:** You have to forgive me, you know.
**NGOZI:** Okay, I forgive you. *(She begins to dress up.)* But you still need God to forgive you. That's what counts….
**KREMI:** God is merciful. So he will forgive me...

## SCENE ONE F

**KREMI:** ... I didn't know I was already... cursed by God without being cursed by the innocent lady until shortly after then... I met a destroyer in the form of a beautiful lady that made me a walking dead...

## SCENE EIGHT

*(The melody continues as Kremi drives along the busy area. A black spirit appears in the bush and changes into*

*a beautiful woman called Horey. She walks majestically to the side of the road and waits. Kremi sees her ahead of him and hurries to stop beside her.)*
**KREMI:** Hello, beauty!
**HOREY:** Hello, handsome!
**KREMI:** You don't mind taking a ride with me, do you?
**HOREY:** Oh not at all, handsome.
**KREMI:** Come on in then. *(Horey enters the car. Then he drives away.)*

## SCENE ONE G
**MOSES:** *(looks shocked.)* The lady is a demon?
**KREMI:** Yes... she is the cause of my condition. Since I slept with her, I've been dying slowly though I didn't know what is wrong with me. I went from one hospital to another... where I was told nothing is wrong with me. I went to a witch doctor who told me what was actually wrong with me....

## SCENE NINE
*(Kemi sits opposite the Witch Doctor in the shrine.)*
**KREMI:** *(looks as if he feels pain as he speaks.)* ... I have been feeling very sick for some times now. I've been to many hospitals but they can't find anything wrong with me except to give me drugs. It's getting worse every day... I decided to consult you, Baba.
**WITCH DOCTOR:** *(makes some incantations and consults the oracle. After a while he looks at him.)* You have slept with a very powerful and wicked demon.
**KREMI:** What does that mean, Baba? I never slept with any demon....
**WITCH DOCTOR:** The oracle says you have slept with a demon while sleeping around.
**KREMI:** Okay, Baba... What must I do to stop this pain.
**WITCH DOCTOR:** *(consults the oracle again before he looks at him, shaking his head.)* I'm afraid there is nothing you can do about it. You have to live with the

pain for the rest of your life....
**KREMI:** Aaaah! Its better to die than to live with this....

## SCENE ONE H

**KREMI:** ... I know one of the reasons I'm in this condition is because of what I did to the innocent Christian lady... So I went to look for her but I was told she has gone to live in United States with her husband....

**MOSES:** Aaah! *(He looks thoughtful for a while before he stands up.)* I'll go and bring my Pastor. If he prays for you, I know you will be well in Jesus name. *(He leaves the room. Soon after he goes out of the room, Kremi gave up.)*

## SCENE TEN

*(Moses opens the door of the room and enter, leading the Pastor inside as the melody continues.)*

**MOSES:** *(gestures at Kremi who is lying lifeless on the bed.)* This is the uncle I told you about, sir.

**PASTOR:** *(frowns and goes to examine him.)* Are you sure this man is alive?

**MOSES:** Yes, sir. He is probably sleeping. *(They move closer to him. When they discover he is dead, Moses begins to screams. The Pastor begins to console him.)*

# THE FATHER OF THE BEAST

## SCENE ONE

*(The car drives towards Beast's house with five men, including Samija and the driver as the melody of "He Who Lives In Glass House" begins.)*

**MELODY:** He who lives in glass house
　　　Must not throw stone at anyone
　　　He who wants to enjoy his peace
　　　Must not look for any trouble…

*(The car enters the compound and stops by the entrance of the house. Four men step down while the driver moves the car to another place. The men move closer to the door, which is opened by another man. Samija looks round the place with curiosity as he is led into the house. The melody continues.)*

## SCENE TWO A

*(Samija and the other men step into the luxurious sitting room. One of them goes inside one of the other rooms and later returns to the sitting room.)*

**1st MAN:** Beast would be here soon, Mr. Samija

**SAMIJA:** Can anyone, please, tell me who this Beast is and what he wants from me?

**2nd MAN:** When he comes, he will tell you everything you need to know.

**SAMIJA:** *(points at the couch.)* Can I, at least, sit down?

**1ST MAN:** *(moves closer to him.)* You don't do or say anything unless he tells you to do so, okay?

**SAMIJA:** What does that mean? Are you guys men of the underworld or something? *(The rest laugh. They are still laughing when Beast enters the sitting room. His face is completely hidden with a pair of big sun glasses, face cap and well trimmed beard. The men stop laughing and stand at attention.)*

**BEAST:** *(in a gruff voice.)* What's happening here, boys?

**1ST MAN:** We are telling the old man the rules. He wants to know if we are men of underworld.

**BEAST:** *(nods thoughtfully.)* I see… *(He looks at Samija,* *gestures him to sit down and then waves at the rest to leave. Samija goes to sit down, looking curious while the rest leave. Beast goes to take a bottle of wine on the shelf.)* Do you care for some drinks?

**SAMIJA:** *(looks uneasy.)* I... em... I don't ... *(Beast frowns at him.)* May be some other time...

**BEAST:** I'll give you some so that you can relax, eh? *(He pours the drink in two glass cups and goes to give one to Samija before he sits down close to him, sipping his.)* Why do you want to know if we are men of the underworld?

**SAMIJA:** I... em ... just want to know.

**BEAST:** Have you heard of me before?

**SAMIJA:** No... no... sir....

**BEAST:** Are you sure?

**SAMIJA:** I'm sure...

**BEAST:** I guess that is the reason you want to know if we are men of the underworld. For the record purpose, we are actually men of the underworld. We are involved in drugs, blood contract, human trafficking, sales of arms and human parts.... *(He shrugs when Samija looks disturbed.)* We supply armed robber weapons and assassinate political figures and make lots of money. We may be people's worst nightmares but we make a hell of money, enjoying our lives at the expense of other people's convenience, pains, sorrows and even deaths. You can consider us as public enemy number one.

**SAMIJA:** *(in a quiet voice.)* Why do you have me brought me here...? I mean I don't have business with you.

**BEAST:** Oh, yes you have business with us - a very good one for that matter.

**SAMIJA:** *(looks puzzled.)* How? I don't possess anything you want, do I?

**BEAST:** Let me tell you a story which will make you understand why you're going to do business with us. *(He pauses briefly before he begins.)* There was once a family who would have been very successful if not for the husband of a hard working woman. The husband was also the father of two responsible boys. Through the effort of this woman, the children were able to go to school until they were planning to go to the University to study medicine and law. This woman did different jobs and even appeal to her family to give her money before she could get enough money to fulfill the dreams she had for her children. The father proved to be very responsible by gambling, drinking and womanizing ...

**SAMIJA:** *(looks stunned.)* Oh, my God!

**BEAST:** I would appreciate it if you don't interrupt me, old man... This man got hold of the money the woman was planning to use to fulfill her sons' dreams and gambled with it....

## SCENE THREE

*(Sammy and Mira are in the shabby sitting room, shouting at each other in anger and frustration.)*

**MIRA:** You can't send your children to school and help them fulfill their dreams to become a doctor and a lawyer. I did all what I can to raise money for their school and, you, irresponsible man went to gamble with it....

**SAMMY:** I don't know what gave you the impression that I took the money

**MIRA:** You are the only one who knew where I kept it! So give me another story!

**SAMMY:** Someone else could have taken it!

**MIRA:** Okay, I know what to do. *(She moves closer to him.)* I'll go to a witch doctor and tell him to strike the person who took the money dead!

**SAMMY:** *(suddenly becomes sober.)* Now, now, don't... don't do that.

**MIRA:** Why not? If I don't see the money, that is exactly what I'm going to do.

**SAMMY:** Okay, okay I'll give you the money next week.

**MIRA:** I need the money now! If you've gambled with the

money, you are a dead man!

## SCENE TWO B

**BEAST:** ... This man denied the children the chances of fulfilling the dreams of becoming a doctor and a lawyer. Even then, this is not the worst thing the man did. The worst was to cause the death of his wife who struggled so much to raise the children into responsible citizens of Nigeria....

## SCENE FOUR

*(Mira is on the sick bed while the two teenage children are beside her, crying as the melody continues.)*

**MELODY:** *He who wants to eat the flesh of others*
*Must always first eat his own flesh*
*He who wants to drink human blood*
*Must always drink his own blood*
*He who wants to pin others with needle*
*Must always pin himself first....*

**MIRA:** *(looks very sick as she speaks in quiet voice)* ... When you went to get me some food... some people came to tell to me about Jesus and they told me if I want God to forgive me all my sins, I should forgive everything your father has done to me.... **(Tears begin to run down from her eyes.)** It was hard for me to do it, but after they led me in prayers, I'm able to forgive him from the bottom of my heart.... I may not... be able to live long to help the two of you fulfill your dreams but I have to tell you that only God can help you in fulfilling your dreams.... No one can... not even I can help you, no matter how much I try except God gives the people the power to help. So it is better you have good relationship with God through Jesus Christ... It's the best you can get from me....

## SCENE FOUR

**BEAST:** ... The poor mother died that day because of the irresponsible father.... **(He stands up, walking**

*round the large sitting room, looking thoughtful while. Samija looks more curious.)* The woman who could have made positive impact on her two sons died. As a result of that, the boys were left to parents themselves. Of course, they joined gangs of hoodlums and then later a group of armed robbers. While robbing a bank, one of the boys was killed and the other boy felt the need to change his profession. And so he got involved in blood contract, meaning that he kills for money. He formed a group of hired killers who waste human lives without discrimination. Of course, there is no way you can get so much involved in this kind of business without making rituals. So he used to sacrifice some animals until he was told he needs to sacrifice one of his parents if he wants to remain in the blood business. If his mother is alive, chances are that he would not have gone this far in atrocities. But the poor woman is dead. So he would have to sacrifice his father. *(He glances at Samija who more disturbed.)* Mr Sammy Samija, I am the son who is nicknamed Beast. You are the father of the beast. You made me whom I am and I need to use you as sacrifice so that my business can flourish....
*(Samija leans backward on the couch in despair.)*
SAMIJA: Oh, my God!


## SCENE FIVE A
*(Samija kneels before the shrine at night, wearing only white wrapper and looking tensed and thoughtful. Five men, including Beast who are also in white wrapper stand round him at the shrine. They face Priest who makes incantations as the melody continues.)*
MELODY: *If you don't want your dream to be scattered,*
　　　　　*don't scatter the dreams of other people.*
　　　　　*If you want your sins to be forgiven,*
　　　　　*you must forgive those who offend you*
　　　　　*If you really want to go to heaven,*
　　　　　*you have to give your life to Jesus Christ.....*

*(Samija looks thoughtful for a while as Priest continues to make incantation, using and being decked with fetish items. Samija looks up and smiles faintly as he recalls an event.)*

## SCENE SIX
*(Evagelist talks with Samija outside the house.)*

**EVANGELIST**:…. Sir, among many others, I will like to tell you three reasons need Jesus Christ in your life. One of them is that everyone has sinned, according to Romans 3:23 and the penalty for our sins according to the same book of Romans 6:23 is eternal death in hell fire as it is interpreted in the book of Revelation 21:8. We therefore need Jesus who died for us and cleanses us of our sins with his precious blood.

The second reason we need Jesus is found in Ephesians 6:12 which says: *"For we do not wrestle against flesh and blood but against principalities, against power, against the rulers of darkness of this age, against spiritual host of wilderness in the heavenly places."* According to this passage, our enemies are not human beings like us. They are invisible devils, wicked and so powerful that no force - not even combined forces of human races can deal with any of them. We all need Jesus to fight this battle for us. If we believe in him, his name alone is more than enough to deal with the combined forces of these devils. The Bible says in Philippians 2:10 and 11, *"At the name Jesus every knee must bow, of those under the earth, and that every tongue must confess that Jesus Christ is Lord to the glory of the father."* The last reason which is the most crucial of them all, we all need Jesus is found in what he said in John 14:2 and 3, telling those who believe in him that we should not let our heart be troubled, probably because of what we are facing in this world. He said he was going to prepare a place for us in eternity so that when we depart from this world, we shall be with him…

## SCENE FIVE B

**PRIEST:** *(looks at Samija and moves closer to him, holding a long dagger.)* The gods are ready to accept you as a sacrifice...

**SAMIJA:** My own God who is Almighty says, *"touch not my anointed and do my prophet no harm....."* Let me warn you, if you don't let me alone, you'll be dead.

**BEAST:** What is that, old man. Are you now a prophet of God or what?

**SAMIJA:** I'm not prophets. I am simply a new creature in Christ. So greater is he that is in me than the gods you want to sacrifice me to.

**PRIEST:** We'll see to that. Oh you, gods… *(He raises up the dagger to strike him with it.)* Here is your sacrifice! *(Before the dagger touches Samija's head, thunder strikes, shaking the whole place. It continues to strike until all of them except Samija becomes lifeless. The melody continues as Samija stands up to examine them. When he discovers that they are all dead, he begins to quietly leave the shrine, looking thoughtful; shaking is head pitifully)*

# THE MELODIOUSLY BAD INFLUENCE

## SCENE ONE

*(J.J girl stands in front of some students in the school with a guitar singing.)*

**J.J GIRL:** *When the sun shines we'll shine together*
*Told you I'll be there for ever*
*Said I'll always be your friend*
*Took an oath I'm a stick it out to the end*
*Now it's raining more than ever*
*But we'll still have each other*
*You can stand under my umbrella...*
*Ella ella eh eh eh} 3 times*
*Under my umbrella} 3 times*
*(Ella ella ella eh eh eh eh eh eh!)*

*(The youths sing with her, dancing while Counsellor watches them, shaking his head with pity.)*

## SCENE TWO A

*(J.J girl is with the Counsellor in the office, sitting opposite each other.)*

**COUNSELLOR:** *(smiles at her.)* Thank you for honouring the invitation to my office.

**J. J GIRL:** You're welcome.

**COUNSELLOR:** I believe you're married, aren't you?

**J. J GIRL:** *(smiles at him.)* No, I'm not married but I have two teenage children.

**COUNSELLOR:** I see. *(He sighs.)* You're invited to inspire the students to be the best they can, isn't it?

**J. J GIRL:** Yeah, yeah!

**COUNSELLOR:** Do you realize what you just did is exact opposite of what you are supposed to do? You just inspire the students to be the worse they can be.

**J. J GIRL:** *(frowns.)* How?

**COUNSELLOR:** We'll let start with the song which you sang. It was composed by Rihanna, right?

**J. J GIRL:** Yeah, yeah. What's wrong with the song?

**COUNSELLOR:** Before I answer the question, let me ask you if you really understand the message in the song.

**J.J GIRL:** Of course, I do. The message is quite clear. Even if you don't get it, you can get it through the video.

**COUNSELLOR:** Now, please, consider me as a layperson who has no faintest idea of what the message is about and explain it to me.

**J.J GIRL:** As you can see, I don't have time to explain anything. Perhaps if you tell me your point, I'll understand it.

**COUNSELLOR:** *(looks thoughtful for a while.)* Well, you need to realize that the song you sang is one of the countless songs that introduce youths into vices, crimes and cultism, denying the existence of God.

**J. J GIRL:** Really? *(She looks amused.)* Can I too ask you a question?

**COUNSELLOR:** Yes, go ahead.

**J. J GIRL:** Are a Christian fanatic or not?

**COUNSELLOR:** Whatever you mean by that...

**J.J GIRL:** I'm sorry if I sound impolite but only religion fanatics talk like that.

**COUNSELLOR:** If we bring religion here, we'll be going off the point. I would, however, simply tell you that I am a Christian. The issue right now is about the message in the song, which is not in line with Nigerian values.

**J. J GIRL:** *(frowns.)* What do you mean by that?

**COUNSELLOR:** How would you feel if I tell you that the song preaches against what Nigeria as a nation stands for.

**J. J GIRL:** I don't believe that.

**COUNSELLOR:** But you know it is against moral conduct, don't you?

**J. J GIRL:** You are still addressing the issue like a religious person. One of the things I don't appreciate is for people to try coerce or force others to stand against what they stand against. We cannot all think the same. You are entitled to your own opinion and beliefs just as I'm entitled to mine and so do others.

**COUNSELLOR:** You do agree with me that we all have common ground like the law and what the society stands for or stand against. The common ground also on boils on the issues of values. *(He leans backward, taking a deep breath and let it out.)* Perhaps if I explain what that song means, you will get the point. Can I explain it?

**J. J GIRL:** Oh, sure. Why not? We are all learning in life.

**COUNSELLOR:** *(smiles at her.)* I think I appreciate that fact. We are all learning. So let me explain so that we can reach a compromise. *(He pauses briefly before he continues.)* When finding the source of bad influence in the society and in the entire world, the analysis of songs like Rihanna's points out that some songs are used to destroyed people's moral values and to deny the existence of God. I thank God that you're familiar with the lyrics of Rihanna's song. The analyses goes this way: When whoever sings the song shines from his or her success, they (meaning the singer and the devil) will both profit from it. He will always be part of the singer. The singer takes oath with the devil by saying, "ella, ella, eh, eh" which means "God no, no..." in different languages. In other words, the singer is saying there is no God or God is not involved in the oath.

**J.J GIRL:** *(looks puzzled.)* Are you sure of this?

**COUNSELLOR:** Yes… Rihana who is in a covenant with the devil is trying to get more people to make covenant with the devil, influencing them not to believe in God, who is depicted in the National Anthem as God of creation. She only used the umbrella in the video as a cover up. There are so many songs like that which are full of subliminal messages with the aim to destroy people's moral values and make as them Godless as she is. This is the message you just passed across to the students of the school. As the School Counsellor, I have to point this out to you and the students.

**J.J GIRL:** *(looks thoughtful.)* Although I read something like once in a publication but I must confess that I didn't take it seriously.

**COUNSELLOR:** Thank God, you're taking it seriously now.

You can still make things right by composing songs that will edify the people or promote values and fear of God instead of ungodliness. *(He pauses briefly.)* I'm curious to know how you come to adopt this kind of lifestyle - I mean how you became a singer and single mother of teenage children.

**J.J GIRL:** *(sighs.)* It is a long story. I don't think I'm in the mood to share it right now.

**COUNSELLOR:** Even if it is going to serve as materials in my counselling job?

**J.J GIRL:** *(takes a deep breath and let it out.)* Okay, I'll tell you and I'll make it as brief as possible... *(She looks thoughtful.)* My parents are the cause of what I am today. They are always at loggerheads....

### SCENE THREE

*(Payne and Lynda are in the room, arguing while J.J girl who is aged six watches them.)*

**LINDA:** All members of your family are all generation of lunatics. So your family name is lunatic. *(Payne looks furious and slaps her Linda on the face. She retaliates. They begin to fight until she was beaten into a coma.)*

### SCENE TWO B

**J.J GIRL:** I lived with domestic violence all the days of my childhood until I became a teenager. I grew up hating my father although my mother also have an equal share of the blame.... *(She looks more thoughtful for a while.)* My background made me feel that marriage is all about fight... So I hate the idea of marriage.... When I got to Secondary School, my friends used to tell me so many good things about their families. I didn't believe them. I taught they were just making up so many story just to impress me. There's this girl then called Seun. She's from a Christian home. She has a lot of influence in my life. She used to tell me about Jesus Christ in my school days then....

## SCENE FOUR

*(J. J Girl and Seun who are teenagers are outside the school talking while the melody of "There Are Ups" begins.)*

**MELODY:** *There are ups*
*There are downs*
*In every good things in life*
*There are ups and there are downs*
*With the enemies of good things*
*Trying to stop you on your way up*
*You can stop them before they stop you....*

**SEUN:** Janet Jagun...

**J.J GIRL:** *(frowns.)* Why calling my full name?

**SEUN:** I have something important to tell you.

**J.J GIRL:** I'm all ears.

**SEUN:** My Pastor once said life is a short journey, which can end at anytime or at any stage of life. No matter how long a person lives, life is still very short. When you compare it with eternity or with the way God sees it, no one lives up to a day because the Bible says 2 Peter 3:8 that one thousand years is like a day in the eyes of the Lord. *(She smiles at her, holding her hands.)* Janet… I love you so much.

**J.J GIRL:** *(in a whisper.)* I know...

**SEUN:** But my love for you is not the best I can give you.

**J.J GIRL:** *(frowns.)* What else could be more than love?

**SEUN:** Love of God is far better and superior to the love of any human. So the best I can give you is to give you Jesus. Even if we are not together again for whatever reasons, you'll still have the best of me if I give you Jesus.

**J.J GIRL:** I know you want me to completely surrender my life to Jesus. Isn't it. *(Seun nods with smiles.)* You know you made me a Christian since we became friends. *(She chuckles and touches Seun's nose.)* Who would be a friend of yours without being a Christian?

**SEUN:** *(holds her hands in hers.)* Janet, I know you've not yet given your life to Christ. I want you to be born again now. That's the only way you can get the best of me...

## SCENE TWO C

**J.J GIRL:** *(looks as if she is moved to tears.)* I became born-again that day. Because of my gift in music, she told me to join the choir. I told her I wont unless she joined. Because of me, we both joined the choir where I learned to be a good singer and composer.

**COUNSELLOR:** You mean you started your music career in the Church?

**J.J GIRL:** *(frowns at the question.)* Yeah… so many good musicians began in their music careers in the Church. The instruments and the congregation are there for us to train with.

**COUNSELLOR:** Oh yes, that's true. How did you suddenly change from the belief you once professed.

**J.J GIRL:** *(looks depressed.)* That's the sorrowful part that made me what I am now... *(Her eyes are filled with tears.)* Seun and I were coming from the Church when this crazy driver drove along. The driver hit us from the back while we were walking home. I was fast enough to jump to one side but Seun was not that fortunate. She landed in the hospital... *(She burst into hysterical sobs.)* I was always in the hospital, praying to God to heal her just as she had taught me....

## SCENE FOUR

*(J.J Girl and Seun are in the Church, sitting together and talking as the melody continues.)*

**SEUN:** ... When you really need something from God so much, you pray... If it looks as if you are not getting answers, pray more and back up your prayers with fasting. Then God will know that you're really serious about what you want from Him...

## SCENE TWO D

**J.J GIRL:** *(sobs the more.)* Everybody knew I prayed that period because I loved her so much....

## SCENE FIVE

*(J.Jgirl is in the hospital, making rounded praying Seun lies on the sick bed with her eyes closed while J.J Girl prays as the melody continues.)*

**MELODY:** *There are so many evil people*
*Who want other people to fail*
*In every good thing they do*
*They know how to bring others down*
*And laugh at them if they fall…*

*(As she prays tearfully, Seun's mother called Mama Seun comes inside the hospital room. She pauses briefly before she goes to tap Janet on the shoulder.)*

**MAMA SEUN:** Janet....

**J.J GIRL:** *(looks startled, drying her tears quickly.)* Oh, Mama, you're back...

**MAMA SEUN:** *(in a quiet voice.)* Yes, you need to take a break now. You need to go home and rest.

**J.J GIRL:** I'm fine, Mama…

**MAMA SEUN:** No, you're not fine. You need rest. You've been staying and praying here for days with little or no rest.

**J.J GIRL:** Mama, let me remain with her until she is on her feet.... *(She burst into another fresh sobs.)* I know she would have done the same for me if I were in her shoe.

**MAMA SEUN:** Your spirit is willing but your body is weak.

**J.J GIRL:** Please….

**MAMA SEUN:** You please.... go home and rest….

## SCENE TWO E

**J.J GIRL:** ….. By the time I returned to the hospital again.... *(She sobs more hysterically.)* My friend and my sister who meant so much to me - who gave me the true meaning of love and true life was dead.... That day was the day I turned my back against Jesus Christ. I switched back into my childhood experiences.

If she was alive, my life would never have been like this. The belief in God which she had instilled in me is still inside me till now despite going deep, deep down into the world. It made me feels that though there is God somewhere but He is nowhere to be found in this world. If not, why didn't He come around when I need Him to heal my precious friend? After all, God knows that I couldn't survive spiritually without her. Why then didn't God come to my aid and heal my friend...? I began to use the gift of music which I developed in the Church through Seun's influence to sing for money. I met some men who used me just as I used them. I resolved that you're better of without any man.

**COUNSELLOR:** *(sighs and stands up quietly to give her some drinks in a small fridge close to him.)* You can have this.

**J.J GIRL:** *(dries her eyes with a small handkerchief.)* Thank you very much.

**COUNSELLOR:** *(pauses for a while before he sits down again.)* Do you know you sacrificed the best thing your friend gave to you when you left Jesus?

**J.J GIRL:** *(looks thoughtful for a while.)* I guess you're right.

**COUNSELLOR:** What that also means is that you betrayed the friend you loved so much, going by what you said.

**J.J GIRL:** *(looks puzzled.)* Oh, no! I don't think so....

**COUNSELLOR:** *(in a gentle voice.)* Let me explain it to you this way. Your friend gave you Jesus, the best of her and influenced you to be a vessel for the Lord. When God took her away from you, you turned against the Lord and use your gift to influence others to turn against God...

**J.J GIRL:** *(looks stunned.)* H-h how?

**COUNSELLOR:** Actually, I wont blame you that much because there are many things, which you didn't understand even up till now. First, she told you she may be separated from you sooner or later, going by what you told me. *(She nods vigorously.)* Secondly, she discovered that you're gifted in music. *(Again she nods.)* The gift, as you know, is from God. It is meant to be used to positively influence others, not to be used to make them deny God as you sang it to the students. *(She nods slowly, looking confused.)* The second thing you're ignorant of is that, as she was departing from this world, she was been welcomed to heaven where, according to the book of Revelation 21:4, God wipes away every tears in the place where there is no more death, nor sorrow, nor crying, nor pain. All you have there is bliss. Nobody can afford to miss that place for any reason. So I will tell you that you must go back to Jesus if you don't want to keep betraying your friend and, most importantly, if you don't want to end up in the lake of fire which is indicated in Revelation 21:8…. *(There is a long silence as J.J Girl looks very thoughtful and sobber. Then she nods.)* Can I pray with you. *(She nods quickly. He holds out his hands. She takes them. He begins to pray with her.)*

## SCENE SIX
*(About a year later, J. J Girl stands before the youths to sing.)*

**J.J GIRL:** As you can see, I'm not a girl. I'm a mother, a Christian and a music minister who is now called Evangelist Janet. I have a great message from the Lord for you through this song titled: "Even Though I Was A Sinner!" *(She begins to sing.)*

*Even though I was a sinner*
*Jesus loves me but I don't know why*
*Even though I sin against him*
*His love for me has never changed*

*Since I know Jesus Christ loves me*
*I will serve him and live my life for him*
*Even though I go through storm of life*

*He has promised to be with me*

*I have given everything to Christ
Because he is my life and my breath
I will do everything to please him
Because he is everything to me.*

# BOOKS BY THE SAME AUTHOR: DIPO TOBY ALAKIJA,
Published By Calvary Rock Publishing and Resources

## The Weight Of Death,
### Dipo Toby Alakija's story Of The Spirit Eyes

PLAY ONE: HORROR IN THE FAMILY: Talimi probably did not envisage his death when he was trying to compel his son, Damola to succeed him in the occult Brotherhood. Other members of the secret cult were aware of the battle between them. So when Talimi died; his family, especially Damola who was a diehard Christian began to fall prey to the cult. Using all their powers and the spirit that posed as Talimi's ghost, the cult waged war against the family, tormenting and making them to be at loggerheads.

PLAY TWO: RITUAL KIDS' KIDNAPPERS: Victor and the rest of the members of the School Bible Club were taught that there are lots of evil people in this world but he did not understand why God allowed him to be among the children that were taken away from their parents. He soon understood that he was to be used by God to rescue other children who did not know that everyone that truly believes in Jesus has the power to overcome evil.

PLAY THREE: THE WEIGHT OF DEATH: Awoseun would not have known the real source of problems of mankind if his father had not given him the power to see demons tormenting the people in different ways. What he was yet to know, however, was the power of light over darkness. When he was caught in crossfire between these powers, he desperately sought for deliverance.

*Please, order for copy or copies of this book through:*
*www.createspace.com/5930230*

## The Redeemer And The Dragon
### The Epic Of Three Kingdoms

Dragon, the king of Doom kingdom gets the legal right to rule over the kingdom of man when First Couple breaks the Law Of Dominion and turns all the mortals into his slaves. When The Father who creates all the kingdoms sends The Redeemer to deliver them, Brethren is selected as one of the few giant warriors that will terrorize Dragon and the rulers of darkness in the decisive battle between Eternity kingdom and Doom kingdom over eternal destinations of the people. Because The Redeemer counts on the mortal warriors called Believers to deliver the rest of the slaves, he equips them with The Word and Comforter who teaches them all things. However, a warrior of Dragon called Ignorance blindfolds vast majority of the people and makes them oblivious of the battlefields in The Flesh, The Mind and The Spirit. Since most of these mortals cannot see beyond their immediate environments, the enemies get the chance to lead them on the path of Doom kingdom which is a place of eternal agony, making the battle on the way to Eternity kingdom of The Father so fierce that only the violent Believers can get to the place.

*Please, order for copy or copies of this book through:*
*www.createspace.com/6098633*

## Footsteps In The Mud
### A 13-Episode Drama Package

The 13-Episode drama book involves Bosede who learnt many wrong things from her parents' conduct and foul language. She was forced to marry Kola when she became pregnant. Using her mother's method to handle her father, she tried to subject Kola to her control. In the course of that, she made life terrible for him. Although her mother tried to warn her of the implications of maltreating her husband but Bosede has grown out of control. Consequently, while looking for peace, Kola was pushed out of the house. He made friends with some guys who taught him the unholy ways of life and influenced him to become a menace in the house.

Junior who was born at time the couple never proved to be responsible parents also learnt wrong things from them. He decided to follow his father's footsteps by taking alcohol when he was in primary school. As if that was not bad enough, he tried to teach other children in the school the madness in his home. A school teacher, however, was able to influence him and his mother by teaching them Christian morals. Even then, Junior was soon caught in the crossfire at home as his father tried to enlist him as a future member of a secret cult that posed as a social club.

*Please, order for copy or copies of this book through:*
*www.createspace.com/5934782.*

## No More Tears To Shed

Kidnappers took Tokunbo away from his grandparents in a city in Nigeria when he was a little boy. A nice woman found him in another town and gave him a false identity. She spoilt him with love, making him to grow into a rebellious teenager that was not appreciated anywhere. When Janet made him a Christian, however, life began to make sense to him until the day he was beaten to the point of death for the offence he knew nothing about. He left the town for the city which, unknown to him, held his true identity and the link to his parents in the United States. To find them was only a question of time.

*Please, order for copy or copies of this book through:*
*www.createspace.com/5947227*

## The Unromantic Love Birds

They were very much in love right from their school days but when they got married and had children, romance became the game Charles' wife refused to play. No matter how much he tried to make her understand the unbearable condition her unromantic attitude has subjected him into, she would not change. Consequently, after enduring for so long, he was forced to look for the women that would make up for her weakness. He unofficially married a beautiful lady of insane jealousy. Though she was ready to give him what was missing in his marriage, it soon dawn on him that he has solved one big problem only to create a bigger one.

*Please, order for copy or copies of this book through:*
*www.createspace.com/5945135*

## Bloodshed In Campus

A poor widow tearfully warned her son, Richard, against joining the bad wagon when he got an admission into one of the Nigerian Universities. He resisted the membership of groups of students, including the Christian Fellowship until he had an encounter with a member of The Black Skulls - a deadly and ruthless secret cult on campus. Before Richard knew what he was up against, the head of The Black Skulls had arranged items for his initiation into the cult. While resisting being initiated, he ran to the Christian Fellowship for help. The leader of the Christian Fellowship dragged The President of Students' Union Government (S.U.G) into the conflict. With the involvement of the S.U.G President, another formidable cult called The Red Eyes felt obliged to team up against The Black Skulls. Then the campus turned into a battlefield and BLOODSHED became the order of the black day.

*Please, order for copy or copies of this book through:*
*www.createspace.com/5928055*

## Ransom For Love
### A Collection Of Three Plays

She accepted his marriage proposal without knowing the kind of person he was. She soon discovered that he was a mean and ruthless guy who was always ready to get whatever he wanted by all means even if he has to pay for it with the lives of others. She was in his bondage, especially when her parents who believed he was a generous and gentleman were on his side. Because she considered the proposal to marry him as a marriage engagement with the devil incarnate, she decided that she would rather die than to share her life with him. Then out of the blues, this passionate gentleman sneaked into her life despite all she did to discourage him. She could not resist his love for her when he offered to set her free from the devil incarnate. Then the battle began - sooner than they anticipated.

*Please, order for copy or copies of this book through:*
*www.createspace.com/5938697*

## The Battle Of The Conquerors

Wickedness takes over the land of Bondage from First Couple and subjects everybody into slavery without giving anybody the chance to be free. Love brings The Redeemer from Eternity and offers the slaves the chance to escape. Wickedness soon declares war and engages everyone in the battle. The Redeemer makes the redeemed people Conquerors by giving them the armour of war and Comforter but Wickedness cannot be undone. He has several thousands of years of experience in the war. So he is quick to recognize the weakness of the redeemed people who are ignorant of their strengths and advantages. Although the Conquerors fight like immutable giants, rescuing victims of war, many people suffer heavy casualties. Since King Wickedness knows that a redeemed person is strong enough to chase one thousand of his warriors at a time, and two would put ten thousand into flight, he enlists as one of his warriors the people's deadliest enemy called Disunity. Wickedness is able to strike the people by making them to fight with one another, turning what is supposed to be their best moments in the battle into tales of woes.

*Please, order for copy or copies of this book through:*
*www.createspace.com/5943542*

## The Insanity Of Humanity
### The Dumbing Down Of Humanity

Man is made to exercise his freewill. The mind of his own and the power to choose between right and wrong, good and evil, light and darkness is about to be washed away through brainwashing. The agents of control dubbed as Secret Government by John Todd (the top Illuninati defector) have put necessary machinery in place to ensure that all human beings are in conformity in their thinking and ways of life, trying to wipe away diversity, which makes each person unique. This book attempts to shed light on how the techniques of mind control are applied through the use of propaganda, education, entertainments, drugs, religions, media and other means of communications. It is the result of research works, some of which are based on findings of various researchers and writers like Wes Penre, Bugger Lugz, Edward Hunter, Hadley Cantril, Herbert Krugman, David L. Robb, Vaughan Bell, Juliana Gomez, Ryan Duffy Vice, Henry Makow, David Nicholls, Fritz Springmeire, Steven Hassan, Renate Thienel, Debra Pursell, Mary Pride and a host of others whose works are acknowledged in this book

*Please, order for copy or copies of this book through:*
*www.createspace.com/5818101*

## Network Bible Club Youth And Adult Story Book
### A Collection Of 26 Stories, 26 Poems 26 Hymn tuned Songs And Bible Lessons

The issue of moral instructions in schools and at homes is threatened with extinction. Consequently, so many youths are involved in prostitution, drug addictions, cultism, fraudulent practices, armed robberies and other crimes. Those who are supposed to be trained as leaders in various walks of life are the ones posing serious threats to many lives. Many parents who fail to add moral values to the upbringing of their children often times breed potential criminals under their roofs without knowing it. Apart from these, many other people negatively influence young ones through the media, music, publications, films, conduct and foul language; making them to lose their moral and family values. This book one just like the rest of other volumes is an attempt to bring back moral instructions into schools and campuses through the use of stories, hymn tuned songs, poems, Bible lessons and class activities. It is designed to assist teachers and ministers in Secondary Schools, Bible Clubs, Churches and Campus Fellowships to teach people, especially youths the Word of God and serves as a school text book in subjects relating to literature, music and other creative works.

*Please, order for copy or copies of this book through:*
*www.createspace.com/5967280*

## Foundation Bible Club A-Z Story Book
### A Collection Of Stories, Bible Lessons, Nursery Rhymes And Songs

An adage says, "a man who builds a house without building his child builds what the child will later sell." Proverbs 22:6 says, "train up a child in the way he should go: and when he is old, he will not depart from it." This book is an attempt to assist parents and teachers to meet up to the challenges that befall them in carrying out this important function in the light of the moral decadence that is prevailing all over the world. The first edition of the book was used by several thousands of teachers, ministers and parents in schools, Churches and homes to build the moral values of young ones. Apart from the stories, songs and Bible passages for the young ones to study, there is a seminar material that is based on the lecture which the author delivered to school proprietors, children ministers and Christian professionals in this volume.

*Please, order for copy or copies of this book through:*
*www.createspace.com/5969489*

## The Young Generation Bible Club Story Book
### A Collection Of Stories, Poems And Bible Lessons

Although this book serves as a follow-up to the stories and lessons in Foundation Bible Club A-Z Story Book, it is a separate academic; evangelical and Ministration tool to reach out and teach young ones in primary and junior high schools. Just like other volumes, it contains stories, songs, poems, Bible lessons and class activities that can be used by parents and ministers at homes, Churches, Schools, Bible Clubs and other Fellowships. It is a manual that assists them in boosting the moral values of children of all age groups in the modern days that are characterized with brainwashing information, ungodly teaching materials and entertainments. Apart from the contents for the young ones, there are also lectures and tips on how to effectively use the book to raise God-fearing children. All the published volumes of the book are used by hundreds of thousands of parents, teachers, ministers and other Christian professionals.

*Please, order for copy or copies of this book through:*
*www.createspace.com/56203448*

## Successful Christianity And Basic Ministries
### A Collection Of Christian Resource Materials

The first question is how Christianity is practiced even in a hostile environment. Next to that is the question about the potentials of Christians in spite of their apparent limitations. The other issues are connected to the successes, deliverance, callings, basic ministries of all Christians and evangelism. Various schools of thoughts have attempted these questions but many answers only portray Christianity as a form of religion instead of a way of life as specified by God. Some answers give room for compromise, hypocrisies, dogmas and denominational doctrines.
The misconceptions about these areas of Christianity have brought about worldliness instead of righteousness and false achievements instead of fulfillment. This book which contains six different subjects had been used to hold seminars at various levels, train ministers and Christian workers in Bible Schools and to equip the Church. It explains in simple terms the seemingly complex issues on practice of Christianity, Potentials, Deliverance, God's Kind Of Success, Evangelism and Basic Ministries of a Christian with Biblical principles, life transforming stories and illustrations.

*Please, order for copy or copies of this book through:*
*www.createspace.com/5947458*

## Christian Ministries And Basic Leadership
### A Collection Of Christian Resource Materials

As it is common to say that the hood does not make a monk, the dignified positions and bogus titles of many Christian leaders in modern days do not really make them Gospel Ministers. This course book - a compilation of five resource materials on Missions And Outreach Ministries, Christian Communication Arts, Christian Leadership, Christian Education Methodology and Ministries Of Improvisations - aims at making every matured Christian an effective minister and leader at their respective homes, in communities and nations. It teaches various ways
Christians can meet up to their responsibilities and commitments as ministers and leaders that reconcile people to God and edify the Body Of Christ, reaching out to souls at the same time. All of the resource materials are in use in Bible Schools like College Of Christian Education And Missions, Churches and other ministries to raise Christian workers, Evangelists, Missionaries and other Ministers that serve at various

levels and leadership capacities.
*Please, order for copy or copies of this book through:*
*www.createspace.com/5953953*

## Christian Communications And Human Resources
### A Collection Of Christian Resource Materials

The world is not in need of those who will fix errors of humanity but in dire need of matured Christians that would use their gifts to communicate the word of God and lead their families, the Church, communities and their countries in the way of righteousness. Very few of them, however, seem to have what it takes to take their positions as leaders and ministers in their spheres despite their God-given potentials. Thus this Course Book - a compilation of five resource materials on Christian Oral Communications, Christian Drama Communications, Christian Musical Communications, Christian Human Resources and Children Evangelism - makes serious attempts to introduce everybody into various creative ministries that are required in the Body of Christ and in the world. It teaches in a simple manner the management of human resources and the ways Christians can use their gifts to reach out to souls through speaking, writing, drama, media, musical and children ministries. The resource materials equip and help individuals to identify their callings, providing Biblical principles and guidelines on how to be effective and productive in the service of the Lord in spite of the hostile environments.

*Please, order for copy or copies of this book through:*
*www.createspace.com/5958272*

## Calvary Rock Resource Booklet One
### The Children Of God And The Slaves

This edition begins with children world where stories like "Ben, The Child Atheist", "Lola And The Bible" and "The Three Brave children" are used to teach children of all age groups about the existence of God and the need to study and obey the Bible. The article: "A critical Debate Between An Atheist Professor And His Christian Student" makes the youths and adults appreciate the passage in Psalm 14:1, which says, "a fool says in his heart, 'there is no God...' " There are study articles like "The supreme God," "The Belief in reincarnation" with the

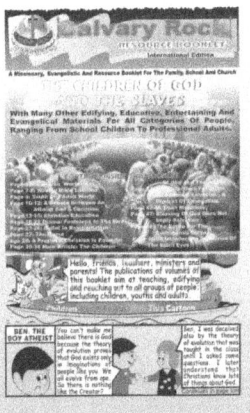

major one: "The children of God And The slaves" which treat the issues of man existing in three parts: The Body, The Spirit and The soul. They expose the readers so the realm of the Spirits. Apart from the drama episode titled: "Going Haywire," there are evangelical materials like "Cheap And Expensive lies", "The woman with four Lovers," "Encounter with Demon from The Grave," "The Life That saves All" and other teaching stories and articles.

*Please, order for copy or copies of this book through:*
*www.createspace.com/5876158*

## The Days Of Gross Darkness
### Calvary Rock Resources Booklet Volume 2

The Children World exposes young minds to things of the spirit through creative use of poems, songs, illustrated stories and Bible lessons. The Youth World is also rich with edifying articles, poems and stories like: "Who Would Share My Burden?" and "Do You Take This Woman As Your Beloved Wife?" The World Of Adults And Christian Professionals begins with the final message of Keith Green who died of plane crash, titled: "Why You Should Go To The Mission Field." The Christian Education Section treats the issue of Christians and Christianity. Next to that is adult story titled: "Lust Affairs" which is the second episode in the drama  book titled: "Footsteps In The Mud." Another story titled: The Land That Has Lost Its Peace" follows the drama. Articles and tracts materials proceed the main subject of "The Days Of Gross Darkness", which extensively teaches and illustrates the spiritually blindness of the modern world in spite of the increase of knowledge. Christian Education And Ministration Services Seminars titled: "Christian Leadership, "Christian Leadership Character", "Patterns; Principles And Power Of Delegation" and "Social Vices Destroy Lives" provide more teaching materials. Other articles and tract materials complement this edi*tion.*

*Please, order for copy or copies of this book through:*
*www.createspace.com/6232521*

www.ingramcontent.com/pod-product-compliance
Lightning Source LLC
Chambersburg PA
CBHW031353040426
42444CB00005B/271